BEING FEMALE: Discovering and Enjoying Your Physical, Emotional, and Sexual Nature

BEING

Discovering and Enjoying Your

PRENTICE-HALL, INC., Englewood Cliffs, N.J.

FEMALE

Physical, Emotional, and Sexual Nature

VERYL ROSENBAUM

Being Female: Discovering and Enjoying Your
  Physical, Emotional, and Sexual Nature by Veryl Rosenbaum

Printed in the United States of America

Prentice-Hall International, Inc., London
Prentice-Hall of Australia, Pty. Ltd., North Sydney
Prentice-Hall of Canada, Ltd., Toronto
Prentice-Hall of India Private Ltd., New Delhi
Prentice-Hall of Japan, Inc., Tokyo

10 9 8 7 6 5 4 3 2 1

Library of Congress Cataloging in Publication Data
  Rosenbaum, Veryl.
    Being female.

    1. Sex   2. Sex (Psychology)   3. Woman-Sexual
behavior. I. Title.
HQ31.R8426   158'.2   73-9843
ISBN   0-13-073601-5

To my sweet husband, Jean, who loves me and with his generous heart makes life delightful.

Contents

I.

THE PROBLEM

What is a woman? And what is it that women really want? These are two important questions. Freud asked the latter one many times and never found the answer. "Despite my thirty years of research into the feminine soul," he said, "I have not yet been able to answer . . . the great question that has never been answered: What does a woman want?"

Through the ages doctors and philosophers, artists and poets, playwrights and novelists have asked what woman is and what she wants. Their answers or suggestions of answers rarely bore any resemblance to the truth. For example, Aristotle said, "Woman may be said to be an inferior man," and in *Hamlet*, Shakespeare wrote, "Frailty, thy name is woman!" On the other hand, Aristophanes asserted, "There is no animal more invincible than a woman, nor fire either nor any wildcat so ruthless," while Coventry Patmore, the nineteenth-century English poet, got around his feelings about women by stating:

A woman is a foreign land,
Of which, though there he settle young,
A man will ne'er quite understand
The customs, politics, and tongue.

But are women really so mysterious? Do they still represent an unknown equation to men? One would not think so considering all that has been written about them and in light of the free exchange between the sexes in contemporary society. Yet the two questions with which this chapter began are precisely those most asked of me by men when I am lecturing. They really do not understand what a female is or what her motivations in life are —a life they are supposedly sharing.

This admission is remarkably poignant, since it is made by one half of the human race about the other half. Equally saddening and disturbing is the fact that many, if not the majority, of females suffer from a similar psychic confusion. They themselves do not know who they are or what their lives should mean.

How did we create such a lack of understanding, not only between men and women but among women as well? With all the capacities with which the human mind is endowed, it is strange that the powers of reason have failed to work in this area.

Actually this muddled state of affairs was not reached overnight; it has taken some time and some doing to achieve it. But the goal of this book is to undo some of the myths that swirl around the female being. They are simply smoke screens that obscure the vision of what the female being is and can be.

Yet I cannot offer any overnight cures for the problems of living a full life as a girl-woman-female person.

I cannot promise a quick, easy formula, for there is no such magic available. If you truly wish to become a complete person, you will have to recognize that there is going to be a great deal of work to do. What happens to you when you learn how to get the most out of total femaleness may look like magic to outsiders, but you will be aware of the work that has gone into the achievement.

If you want your daughter to blossom into a mature, loving, and lovable woman, that task also entails work and responsibility, for it means that you will have to pay attention to her inner life. Most of us learn easily enough how to handle the physical needs of the infant, the growing child, and the maturing adolescent. The real challenge to you, as a mother and as a woman, is meeting the *interior* needs of your developing child.

And you yourself can still become a beautiful person. I use the word "beautiful" in the sense of personality structure and response, for that is where real beauty is found. Nor is it too late for you to change neurotic patterns of thinking or behavior into healthy ones. If you are willing to study and exert your psychological powers, all this good can happen to you!

As I stated at the outset, however, there is no magic formula, no shortcut method. Cinderella stories to the contrary, it is no use to sit around waiting for someone to offer you the wonderful world of complete womanhood in one easy lesson. This is just as unrealistic as believing that if you buy and use the perfect deodorant or mouthwash, you will make some man love you forever. Any happy endings in your life will have to come through your own efforts.

I can offer you an opportunity for joy in living as a

female. Your share of the bargain is that you will have to think and work on your own behalf if you want the reward of being able to live each day with exciting fulfillment.

Being a complete female creates a special serenity that carries you through everyday living and touches all of your activities with grace. And it makes you need to and able to love a man fully. It brings understanding and intuitive knowledge into all your relationships. It makes you an unforgettable person.

Being a complete female gives you strength of purpose and the necessary courage to handle life's difficult situations. It allows you to use your innate aggression for good works, whether as a mother rearing children to be loving people or as a celibate devoting her life to religion. Whether you are a mother, a teacher, an artist, a writer, dentist, scientist, or maid does not matter. What does matter is not *what* you do for a living, but *how* you do it. Earning a living or pursuing any interest or avocation is fascinating when life is focused through the lens of womanliness.

In our country we have an enviable record of women who have achieved prominence in their chosen work and have also fulfilled themselves as women. To mention but a few—Jane Addams, the noted social worker who founded Hull House in Chicago and was, in addition to her social work, known for her efforts on behalf of women's rights and world peace; Eleanor Roosevelt; Georgia O'Keeffe, famed American artist; Helen Hayes; Dr. Helen Taussig, who helped solve the blue-baby disease by perfecting new surgical techniques.

There has always been room in this country for the

woman who wanted to achieve. However, achievement has only been possible when the woman has also achieved personal unity. It is powerful to be whole, because you have an inner sense of assurance that enables you to use your abilities and strengths. It is a poem to be a complete woman. When you have achieved that totality, it becomes the stable center of your being.

Every woman has the capacity to become herself in all of her beauty and grace. There is nothing to stop your growth—except yourself. You make the decision about how much you will grow and how soon.

Too often people establish arbitrary limits for their mental and emotional growth. They automatically assume, for example, that the end of schooling is the end of learning, or that growing as a person ends at a certain stage. Sometimes an event such as marriage is taken as a signal for the end of change and growth. In that sense many people end their lives wastefully early. They may live to the chronological age of seventy-five or more, but their spirit dies while they are in their twenties or thirties.

Think of life as a precious gift, and then think about what you are doing with that gift. What are you doing with your gift of life? Is it a meaningful experience rather than a mere existence, simply making sure you get through each day? Simply existing means that you never really get to the heart of yourself and the heart of life. A meaningful experience means giving all you have to living every single day.

If you think it is too hard to concentrate on living and more fun to be lazy and let life slide by, then you will always be missing a vital part of your life. You will be an empty vessel which is unfulfilled by growth or love. You will die without ever having really lived. What a tragic waste! So let us begin to understand that wonderful, complex creature that is called the female.

It is my earnest wish that as many men as women will read and learn from this book. For if we are going to be complete women, then it follows that we must have complete men around us so that life may be all that it should be for us and for them.

In my experience as a therapist and lecturer, I have noticed how many men are deeply curious about women. And not just curious about women in general but often about their own girlfriends or wives as well. Many men, however, are afraid to admit to their interest, fearing that if they do, they will appear weak and dependent. They hide their curiosity rather than acknowledge that they themselves were once completely dependent upon their mothers for love and for life itself.

Indeed, the majority of men would rather develop and maintain clichés about females, and through that means, avoid understanding women. The average man would rather maintain a convenient stereotype of women than really know the woman he is most intimately involved with. That is not really a very intelligent response to today's world. The roles of men and women are constantly changing and expanding. The impacts of technology, overpopulation, and shifting moral and social issues all combine to alter the parts people must play.

We must learn to know ourselves as well as each other if we are to make our lives more livable. It is time for men and women to stop taking sides against each other. It is time to explore the depths of living and loving together as a unit. We are not separate—man and woman. We are different in sexual development and characteristics, but the seed of life within is the same.

We are men and women of the human race, and we share the capacity to think, reason, talk, plan, feel, hope, and love. In our various intellectual and emotional experiences we are unique on this planet. Yet despite the strong similarities, we live in a climate in which alienation and suspicion flourish. The basic reason for that alienation is fear of the unknown. But it is not just fear of the unknown opposite sex. It is also the fear of another unknown—ourselves, and in particular, ourselves in relation to the opposite sex. It is strange and sad that two halves of a whole should fear each other.

The major fear seems to be that of being hurt and misunderstood by the other sex. But that fear exists only among those who are afraid to grasp the idea of male and female as two halves of a necessary whole. If you were to truly understand yourself as a woman and if the man in your life were to comprehend what being a female is, then you would be able to become whole together.

Why, when completeness is so desirable and adds so much to the personality and enjoyment of life, do some women ignore it or even fight against it? Some women are fearful of knowing themselves better because they had neurotic parents who evidenced negative attitudes toward femaleness. Early in their lives, therefore, these women drew the logical conclusion: If being a girl is bad, then being a woman is worse!

One of my patients, Marie N., had had two unhappy marriages. She generally had difficulty in getting along with men on business levels as well as socially. Although basically an attractive woman, Marie played down her natural feminity. She looked unhappy. She dressed in a severe, colorless style. Yet she longed to be a woman and to be able to respond naturally to men.

Why did Marie have such ambivalent feelings about men? Why was she unable to assume her role as a woman?

Both of Marie's parents had contributed to her inability to understand and accept herself as a woman. Her father had shown by words and actions that he considered women second-class citizens and of little more than nuisance value in the world. He frequently expressed regret that she was not a boy. Marie's mother also downgraded women. In addition, she continually emphasized the unpleasant aspects of being a female and took every opportunity to tell Marie about some incident in which a woman was insulted just for being a woman. Marie was conditioned by her parents to feel sorry for herself because she had the "misfortune" to be born female rather than male.

"My mother's favorite expression was 'It's a man's world' and she used it to cover all kinds of situations from sex to religion," Marie said. "I soon developed a fear of men because they had so much power. I also felt hostile toward them because they were, so I had been taught, so much better than I could ever be. Looking back at my two marriages I can see now where my feelings of fear, hostility, and envy kept me from being a happy and successful wife."

Fear is a disabling emotion. It inhibits growth and checks your ability to venture into the stream of life. You become a hesitant bystander. If you are fearful, it is easy to convince yourself that you are better off avoiding life. You rationalize that in this way you can be safe and secure and you cannot be hurt. Yes, it may be safe, but it is also lonely. Giving into fear is to be willing to lead an emotionally impoverished life. Facing up to fear and learning to know yourself are essential to living a fulfilling life.

There are a number of benefits in being a woman. For example, all humans, male and female, have certain emotional responses and psychological drives in common, but only women have been allowed to develop and utilize these emotions. A woman is expected to be able to understand other people because society allows her to use her intuitive reasoning. But the so-called feminine intuition is a *human* characteristic, not an exclusively female characteristic. Infants are born with this perceptive ability we call intuition. They instinctively recognize and respond to love, dislike, or danger. In our society, however, it has become customary to denigrate intuition in men and discourage its use.

One man told me that he depended a great deal on his wife's intuition in his business affairs. "Why don't you also use your own?" I asked. He looked embarrassed at my suggestion and replied with an uneasy laugh, "You know, men don't have intuition. That's what makes women so different."

Had he been willing to listen, I would have explained to him that what makes women "different" is not their intuition but the fact they they use it. For example, the man to whom I was talking was a successful businessman with years of experience in his field. He had, therefore, accumulated knowledge and experience which, when used in conjunction with his intuitive perceptions, would

17

have enabled him to make his business even more successful.

Boys are also discouraged, of course, from exhibiting gentleness, kindness, or sensitivity, whereas those characteristics are praised in girls. "Where have I failed?" asked one father, deploring the fact that his son was not aggressive enough to please him. He insisted that his son learn habits of hostility and destruction in order to survive in "the dog-eat-dog world."

In insisting on the traditional view that sensitivity is to be discouraged as "sissy" in males and encouraged only in females, men are being cheated of their full emotional life. But as long as this prevails, it can be said that full and complete emotional development is one of the advantages of being a woman.

There are some very practical advantages to being a woman. Although thought of as the weaker sex, women actually have fewer major diseases and a longer life span than men.

In sexual matters, women have another advantage. Unlike men, they do not have to have an orgasm in order to conceive. A man's orgasm is not only necessary for reproduction, it is also limited in length (from ten to forty seconds). A woman's orgasm is purely for pleasure, and in the sexually mature female it can be prolonged for as long as an hour.

Yet until recently the primary lesson taught to women was that men were the superior beings and women at best were second-class. Even Freud failed to understand the advantages of being a female. He coined the phrase "penis envy," believing that women must be envious of the male sex organ. His reasoning was that if men had more than women, women must therefore feel deprived.

But let us not be too critical of Freud. He lived in a period when women were just beginning to assert themselves, and he was an old man (he died in 1939) by the time changes started to be made. In a very real sense he was the historical prisoner of the social times in which he lived. Had he lived today his view of women and their roles might well have been different. The work Freud could not do was begun by his student Marie Bonaparte, whose book *Female Sexuality* is a master text for students of psychoanalysis. She initiated objective study of the psychology of women and their place in society.

No, most women do not have a desire to have a penis. But after centuries of being brainwashed into thinking that they should want to change places with men, many of them came to believe it was a good idea. Actually, when men are psychoanalyzed there often emerges a deep envy of women. Their envy is usually based on the fact that it is women who sustain life. Unconsciously men believe that their role is relatively insignificant. Any man can impregnate a woman, but only a woman can grow life and afterward sustain that life with her body's milk. In order to compensate for their feelings of inferiority, men have tried to avoid the issue by accusing women of being inferior and of wanting male sexual organs. That is not an unusual behavior pattern. We often accuse others of having faults that we believe we have, because we do not want to acknowledge our own feelings about ourselves.

The accusation that women envy male sexual power

has contributed to the alienation between the sexes. That is a high price for men as well as women to pay for soothing the male ego. Yet women have contributed to the cost by accepting the premise that men are to be envied. That is why so many women continue to suffer from loneliness, despair, and a variety of neurotic symptoms. In the midst of increasing sexual freedom, they suffer from frigidity. During a time of increased equality in relationships, they are unable to love or accept love.

Historically there are good reasons why women have believed they were inferior beings. For centuries women were regarded by men as mere chattel, suitable only for performing certain domestic tasks including bearing and raising children. A woman lived a life of servitude in which she was denied the right to own property, to vote, to hold office, and so on. She was absolutely dependent, first upon her father, then upon her husband. Of course, it was not an entirely black picture, for women were a necessary part of the economic scheme before the Industrial Revolution. A married couple usually worked side by side, raised their family as a team, and shared all aspects of their hardworking life.

Many changes were brought by the industrial Revolution. First men went to work in the new factories, and the old partnerships of husband and wife were no longer economically viable. Soon the rapid spread of industrialization drew women and even children into the lower strata of the labor market. Later, under more enlightened social customs, children were no longer permitted to work but were sent to school, but the old unity of the home had vanished and women were left outside the mainstream of the new competitive world.

Until the end of World War II, women were at best looked upon as asexual beings. "Nice" girls, it was thought, did not have sexual feelings or desires. It was men who were passionate, not women. Indeed it was commonly believed that women could not experience sexual pleasure. Those women who did experience any sexual feeling were made to feel there was something shamefully wrong with them. Medically they were considered freaks, and morally they were outside the pale.

Today we are facing a crisis in male-female relationships and unless women are willing to accept themselves as whole females, their social and political gains will not add to their happiness.

Too many of today's women's liberation goals are still pegged to male goals. Too often women confuse liberation from male dominance with becoming pseudomen. Replacing male domination with male orientation will not solve the basic problem of female insecurity. Understanding the true nature of femaleness and reconstructing one's life accordingly is *real* liberation.

It is common sense, as well as morally right, that women should have equal pay for equal work and equal rights in terms of legal and economic questions. But one of the interesting aspects of life is that men and women are emotionally and sexually different from each other. Women must understand that and recognize it as a positive value.

II.

THE FEMALE
BODY

For thousands of years writers and philosophers have rhapsodized about the human body. In the eighteenth century Julian Offroy de la Mettrie wrote, "The human body is a watch, a large watch constructed with . . . skill and ingenuity." "If anything is sacred," Walt Whitman declared, "the human body is sacred." And Alfred North Whitehead poetically defined the human body as "an instrument for the production of art in the life of the human soul."

Yet it is a constant source of amazement to me, even in this era of enlightened sex education and general female liberation, how little understanding women really have about their bodies, particularly their sexual parts. Furthermore many women have little or no curiosity about their bodies other than to be concerned about their weight and the onset of wrinkles. This lack of interest is a continuance of the Victorian attitude that "ladies" should not be well informed about their physiology and sexual make-up.

But times have changed and ignorance is no longer justified. We now know that the functions of the body and how you as an individual react to them compose part of your personality structure. Therefore let us examine the female body with both interest and wonder, for it is a beautiful as well as a complicated structure. The more you know about your body, the easier it will be for you to live comfortably with it.

The largest cell in the human body is the female egg, yet it is only about one quarter the size of a period mark. Indeed, the egg is fifty thousand times larger than the sperm from the male. Millions of spermatozoa may reach an egg, but only one, if any, penetrates it.

At the moment of conception the egg and sperm fuse to form one cell. Egg and sperm each contain only a half set of chromosomes, the elements which transmit inherited characteristics, and when egg and sperm join to create one cell, that cell then has the genetic material needed to make a unique human being.

The sex of an embryo is determined by the type of sperm that fertilizes the egg. Sperm that create boys have a special sex chromosome called Y. Sperm that create girls carry the sex chromosome X; in addition, the mother's egg is always X. At conception the cell that will become a girl child is the combination XX; the cell that is to be a boy child is the combination XY.

Generally the XY chromosome combination carries with it certain disadvantages and built-in frailties. Males have a greater tendency to die than do females, particularly during infancy and again in the later years. Because the XY chromosome is not as strong as the XX combination, males are prone to hemophilia and color blindness, both rare conditions in females. So you see, even from the instant of conception, the female is endowed with certain strengths.

It is helpful to note the similarities and differences in the sexual development of the male and female fetus. Sometime during the second month in the womb an enlargement occurs at the lower end of the fetus's digestive tract. This enlargement is the cloaca, and from it develop the rectum, bladder, and external genital organs. The bladder becomes divided from the rectum by a thin wall, and the external genitalia are formed at the end of the digestive tract tube.

A swelling known as the genital tubercle appears at the front opening of the tube. From this develop the glans penis in the male and the clitoris in the female.

The penis is composed of spongelike erectile tissue and a bulblike extremity called the glans. The glans is covered by a foreskin and contains an opening which marks the end of the urethra, the tract through which urine is released. During ejaculation the semen or sperm is also passed through this tube and opening.

The clitoris is part of the female genitals and, like the penis, is made up of erectile tissue. It, too, has a head with a foreskin covering it, although both remain much smaller than the male glans and foreskin.

At the opening of the cloaca, the enlargement at the end of the digestive tract from which develop the rectum, bladder, and external genitals, there are two folds which grow backward toward the interior of the body. In the male these folds meet to enclose the urethra, the small tube leading from the bladder through the penis to the tip of the glans.

In the female these folds do not meet but become the

forerunner of the labia minora, the inner lips that surround the opening of the vagina and urethra.

At the side of each of these folds there develops a swelling. In the male these become the two halves of the scrotum, the pouch of skin that contains the testicles and lies behind the penis. In the female these swellings form the labia majora, the outer lip of the vulva which is the female genital orifice.

Aside from these physical sexual characteristics, there are only slight differences at birth between a male and a female child. The pelvic structure of the female is larger than the male's in order to accommodate the children she may later bear. Her knees and elbows are more knocked to make it easier for her to someday hold her baby, the elbows enabling her arms to form a kind of cradle, the knees stabilizing her stance.

The sizes of individual children depend primarily on inherited characteristics, but generally speaking, girls are smaller than boys in terms of general bone structure and muscle development.

When looking at a naked young child from behind it is impossible to tell its sex. Male and female body development shows little apparent difference until puberty. However, puberty can begin as early as nine years of age, especially among girls, who frequently begin their puberty growth a year or so before boys.

The changes that take place at puberty begin with the pituitary gland located deep within the skull at the lower part of the brain. The pituitary gland is a part of the body's endocrine system. This system is composed of glands in various parts of the body, each of which secretes a specific hormone into the bloodstream.

These hormones regulate many of the body's functions, and during puberty they are part of a chain reaction that results in many physical changes.

The sex glands are called gonads. The female's gonads are her ovaries, two almond-shaped glands, one located on each side of the uterus. The uterus, or womb, is situated at the upper end of the vagina.

During puberty the ovaries receive a hormone from the pituitary gland and begin to mature. The ovaries themselves then secrete hormones that cause a number of overall physical alterations. With this maturation of the female reproductive system comes the development of the secondary sex characteristics that begin to change the appearance of a girl into that of a woman.

The first sign of these changes is the growth of the breasts. Nipples grow out slightly, and the dark circles, or areolas, around the nipples puff up. The nipples feel very sensitive, and in some cases are actually painful during this period. This is not a cause for alarm, however, but is merely a symptom of the maturation process.

Each woman differs in breast size and shape. Despite the blandishments of the advertising world, there is no "perfect" shape or size. From a biological point of view, it does not matter how big or how small the breast is, as breasts of any size can produce milk for the nurturing of infants. And for the emotionally mature woman the size and shape of her breasts is of little consequence, as real sex appeal is generated far more by what is within her than by any physical characteristic.

While a female's breasts are budding, her hips also begin to round out as a result of the broadening of the bony pelvis and the deposition of subcutaneous fat. Her legs lengthen, thus changing body proportions. During mid and late adolescence, pubic and auxiliary hair appear. Other changes include the further development of the labia and clitoris. Skin secretions change, and the sweat glands become hyperactive, which is why acne is so common during adolescence.

Sometime between the ages of ten and sixteen the young girl begins her menstrual period. Technically it is called the menarche, and its onset is a most significant event in the female individual's development. It is the mark of the physical journey from childhood to womanhood.

Menstruating is, of course, a normal human function, despite all of the weird myths and folktales that have grown up around it. Truthfully, it is hard to say that this particular female body function is a "beautiful experience." It is more honest to admit that it can be a nuisance to bleed every month, but that's all it is—a minor nuisance. If you usually have painful or uncomfortable menstrual periods, you should be examined by your physican to determine if there is something physically awry. A physiological or organic basis for menstrual discomfort, however, is relatively uncommon, and because menstruation is a normal function of the female body, the cramps that often accompany it are almost always based on emotional difficulties. These difficulties are usually centered around the supposed problems of being a female, which I will discuss in detail in later chapters.

When a girl is born, her ovaries contain the seeds for approximately four hundred thousand eggs, all that she will have in her lifetime. She is more than abundantly supplied, as only about four hundred of these eggs will actually be released during the fertile periods of her life. Each month after menstruation begins, the pituitary gland sends out hormones which are carried through the bloodstream to the ovaries. The hormones cause one of the ovaries to begin ripening an egg. (The ovaries usually alternate in ripening eggs.)

As the egg in the ovary ripens, the uterus lining thickens and stores up blood. The thickened lining is meant to serve as a bed for the fertilized egg, and the stored-up blood is for its nourishment. This process is an act of preparation and precaution by nature just in case there is going to be a male around to do the fertilizing.

After the egg is ripened, it is released from the ovary. This releasing of the egg is ovulation, and it occurs about halfway through the twenty-eight-day reproductive cycle, or approximately fourteen days after the beginning of the previous menstrual period.

When the egg leaves the ovary, it is caught in the Fallopian tube nearest it. The egg floats down this tube toward the uterus, at which point it can be fertilized by the propelled sperm. If fertilized, the egg lodges itself in the thickened lining of the uterus.

If, however, the egg is not fertilized, it shrivels up and continues down the Fallopian tube. The enriched lining of the uterus is not needed if the egg goes unfertilized, so it begins to shrink and in the process it sheds its extra store of blood. This blood leaves the uterus through the vagina, and the unfertilized microscopic egg leaves the body along with the unneeded blood.

The amount of menstrual flow, the number of days of flow, and the days between periods vary greatly among individual women. Whatever your cycle is, it is probably normal for you.

When a girl first begins to menstruate, her periods and flow may be irregular. This happens because the hormone secretion which regulates the cycle takes time to become established. At first the hormones from the pituitary gland are usually too weak to stimulate the ovary to release an egg monthly. Repetition of the hormone action eventually makes the signal stronger and finally stimulates the ovary into releasing a ripened egg. Thus a girl may actually begin ovulating a few months to a year after her first menstrual peiod.

During menstruation only about one-half cup of blood is passed from the body, along with some tissue and watery fluids. That is not enough to weaken a woman or to lower her resistance to illness. The old idea of the menstrual period being, as one patent medicine advertisement used to put it, "the difficult days" is simply not fact. It is a fallacy that menstruation incapacitates a normal girl or woman.

The monthly reproductive cycle continues in the female until her forties or fifties, when she experiences menopause. Menopause marks the end of her ability to conceive and bear children, and once again changes take place in the body, this time adjustments to the end of the egg-producing cycle.

The menopause does not have to be unpleasant or uncomfortable. As with menstrual cramps, most of the problems associated with menopause are usually emotional in origin.

The major physical change during this period is that the glands secrete less estrogen. This causes the menstrual cycle either to stop abruptly or to end gradually. The latter effect appears to be most common, and such a tapering-off period may last for a year or for several years, depending upon the individual. During this time many women experience "hot flashes," waves of warmth or rather intense heat that sweeps over the body. A woman having a hot flash may perspire and appear red in the face during the few minutes that the feeling persists. These hot flashes stop when the menopause is complete and the hormonal equilibrium is reestablished within the body.

If a woman feels great physical discomfort during menopause, she can obtain relief by replacement therapy with estrogen. Many gynecologists today begin permanent estrogen replacement therapy at the onset of menopause. This not only completely prevents discomfort, but it also prevents early aging. It counters protein loss and helps to keep breast tissue firm. In general, the aging process slows down. While estrogen replacement is fairly new in medicine, there is some evidence that such treatment lessens the chances of cancer of the genital tract and the breasts.

It is important to note that menopause is simply a physical state and signifies the end of menstruation and the ability to produce children. With or without estrogen replacement therapy, menopause is not the end of anything else in a woman's life. It has nothing whatever to do with a fe ale's ability to experience sexual pleasure or with her ability to give sexual pleasure. In a later chapter I will discuss the emotional implications of the menopause.

In addition to the changes that take place during puberty and menopause, the other main changes in the female body occur when the woman is pregnant. The first indication of pregnancy is the cessation of the menstrual period. Some women also feel a tingling and enlargement in their breasts. Another common indicator is more frequent desire to urinate, caused by the enlarged uterus pressing on the bladder.

As with menstruation, there has developed a whole body of myths associated with pregnancy. As a result, some women suffer needless fears and anxieties. Many women fear that at the end of their pregnancy they will be left with sagging breasts, varicose veins, and weak abdominal muscles. Many women also think that being pregnant means getting fat and staying fat. Yes, any of these things can happen if a woman refuses to follow a sensible and simple health plan during her pregnancy. They are what are called preventable complications.

To safeguard her body and the health of her unborn children, a woman should be informed about the changes that take place inside herself during pregnancy. She will then be better equipped to cope with the total experience of pregnancy.

During pregnancy the glands of the breast change under the influence of estrogen and progesterone hormones. As the breasts enlarge, they become heavier—sometimes by as much as one pound. Gravity naturally pulls them down, and their supporting tissue is strained and stretched. This, in turn, can cause the breasts to sag. The preventive measure for breast sag is to wear a good expanding brassiere especially made to give pregnant women the muscle support they need. The large-breasted woman should wear it day and night.

Because the blood in the veins of the legs has to flow up against gravity, the veins have valves which prevent a backward flow of blood. If the upward pumping is hampered in any way, the weight of the blood in the veins causes the valve below to give out. The result is varicose veins.

In pregnancy the extra downward pressure of the enlarging uterus places an additional burden on the blood vessels, and that, in turn, increases the possibility of varicose veins developing. There is a way, however, of helping to prevent varicose veins.

The upward flow of blood is helped by the activity of leg muscles. Simple and gentle exercising of the toes, feet, and legs serves to benefit the blood flow. Elevating the legs while sitting or lying down also aids circulation. If a woman does get varicose veins during her pregnancy, she should wear support stockings to help relieve the pressure on her legs. After the baby is born, however, and the additional pressure on the legs is eliminated, varicose veins resulting from pregnancy usually disappear.

To prevent stretched abdominal muscles, good posture is essential. And stretch marks can be avoided by rubbing the stomach skin with warm olive oil.

All of these precautions are easy to take. They do not require much money, but they do require some time and personal attention. However, the results are well worth it.

Obesity is the trap too many pregnant women fall into. Using the old adage, "I have to eat for two now," some women make their pregnant condition an excuse to indulge in a nine months' eating binge! Obesity is as easy to prevent in pregnancy as it is when not carrying a child. People who are overweight have emotional problems, and that applies to pregnant women as well.

The overall weight gain during pregnancy should be no more than twenty-five pounds. This gain consists, on the average, of the following weights:

Fetus—7 pounds
Placenta—1 pound
Amniotic Fluid—2 pounds
Increased Weight of Uterus—2 pounds
Increase in Blood Volume—4 pounds
Extra Cellular Fluid—4 pounds
Increased Breast Weight—1 pound
Stored Protein—4 pounds

There is no correlation between the weight gain of the mother and the baby's weight at birth. The baby draws his nourishment from the mother, so the pregnant woman should be on a well-balanced diet, high in protein.

Because of the increased hormonal excretions during pregnancy, other physical changes occur, including an enlargement of the thyroid gland, the raising of the diaphragm, darkening of the skin around the areolas of the breasts, and a darkening of the enlarged nipples. Of course the most obvious change is the growing size of the uterus.

A woman who is pregnant can usually lead a normal physical life, and she should do so if she is able. She may continue to work and play as she wishes, as long as the activity does not exhaust her. She may also continue to have sexual intercourse until the time her doctor suggests she stop, which is often at seven months. Some physicians, however, believe that healthy pregnant woman can have *gentle* intercourse until the time of delivery. Gone are the days when pregnancy was equated with weakness. It should be a very healthy time of life. Many of the problems surrounding pregnancy stem from emotional difficulties. These will be discussed in a later chapter, as I have tried here to simply present the "body facts." Of course it is impossible to separate the mind and the body in actual living, because in order for life to be lived fully the body and mind should be in harmony. It is important, however, to know your body from an objective point of view and to understand how it is designed to function.

III.

THE PSYCHOSEXUAL DEVELOPMENT OF MALE AND FEMALE

In order to become an emotionally mature person, the life journey through infancy, childhood, and adolescence must be traveled successfully. There are certain events which every human being experiences and which taken together are categorized by psychoanalysts as "psychosexual development." No one is really aware of these psychological happenings when they are actually being experienced in childhood, but they do occur.

The psychological progress of the human being from infancy to adulthood is truly fascinating, and it is not so complicated that one need be a professional therapist to grasp the basic facts.

A mature person is one in whom the components of his or her psychological being are in harmony. For convenience of discussion, these components are classified by the terms *id*, *ego*, and *superego*.

The id refers to repressed memories and the instinctual drives, such as aggression and sexual desire. The ego is one's sense of self, which includes conscious memories.

It is the ego that you use directly in dealing with the external world. In fact, the ego is a kind of middleman between the external world and your own internal world of thoughts and feelings. The superego, on the other hand, consists of your personal system of ethics. It sits like a judge over your choices in life, whether, for example, to steal or not, whether life is meant to be enjoyed or suffered through.

Every infant is born in a state of pure id, for the ego and superego are not developed prenatally. Therefore a baby comes into the world demanding immediate satisfaction of his needs, because he has no internal mechanism that allows him to be patient, considerate, or loving. He is all instinctual drive to remain alive, and he has but one instrument with which to draw attention to himself and his needs. That instrument is his mouth, and the expression itself is crying.

This beginning stage of life is called the oral phase, and it lasts approximately fifteen months. It is probably the most crucial period in an individual's life, male or female. During the oral phase the infant is totally dependent upon his mother or some other adult to care for and nurture him. How a child is handled in this stage will affect him for the rest of his life. If a baby is loved and satisfied during the oral period, he will easily move on to the next stage of the growing process. If he is not satisfied during the oral period, he will always seek gratification on that level of maturity and never grow up emotionally, even though his body will be fully developed into physical maturity.

To enable the child to survive, he is born with the ability to suck, and throughout the oral stage his sensory impressions are largely centered around his tongue and mouth. As the infant begins to reach out for objects, he will try to relate them to his sensual mouth. Everything in his world is to suck, and it is amusing to watch a baby discover his toes and then proceed to see if they will fit into his mouth.

Many people are offended when psychologists say that a baby has sexual feelings. That is because people mistakenly think that those feelings are centered in the child's genitals. Perhaps "sensual" is a more appropriate term to explain the infant's body feelings.

Sensual sensations are extremely pleasant. They are sought by infants as well as adults because they give pleasure and reduce tension. The oral stage is a time of sensual attachment by the mouth, through which the child is not only nurtured but gains pleasure through the act of sucking. When a woman is breast-feeding, the child receives most of the milk during the first four minutes of nursing. But nature continues to provide a trickle of milk for at least fifteen or twenty minutes longer in order to satisfy the infant's oral need to suck. There is no sight more beautiful than that of a baby fast asleep at the breast, completely orally satisfied.

Much more than sucking, however, is involved in the beginning stage of development. The mother's attitude is of primary significance. She will have particular feelings about her child and herself and will treat the baby in a way that reflects her attitude.

June always wanted a baby girl. As a child she had been loved by parents who thought being female was wonderful. Her father particularly wanted a daughter because he liked and admired women and thought it was a sad thing to bring up a son only to later see him go off to war. June grew up feeling delight and approval in her femininity, and she was eager to pass that feeling on to a daughter of her own.

I believe that breast-feeding is important for babies. It is apparent that by providing lactation, nature intended for the mother and baby to be very close during the first year of the child's life. Further, a nursing baby is able to feel his mother's warm skin against his face, to experience the mother's natural body odor, and to feel her heartbeat as he did while in the womb. That is probably why breast-fed children generally are more content than bottle-fed babies. In addition, they usually have fewer childhood diseases and are, on the whole, more relaxed.

An infant in the oral, id stage does not know that it takes five minutes to heat a bottle of milk, because he does not think and has no comprehension of time. He only feels that his whole body is hungry RIGHT NOW. Those five minutes necessary to heat a bottle must feel like an eternity to a hungry baby. A nursing mother, however, can be there immediately with just the right temperature of milk and her warm, loving body.

From the first moment of life outside the womb the child's ego begins to grow. Although he has no intellectual awareness of what is happening to him during the oral stage, every feeling directed toward him by the mother and the ways in which he is satisfied or frustrated are stored in his growing unconscious.

The id, ego, and superego contain vast areas that are unconscious. And I do mean *completely* unconscious. The individual is unaware of his unconscious process, but is nevertheless controlled by it. People cannot consciously recall their oral stage of development because it occurred before they developed conscious thought and the ability to conceptualize and verbalize. However, all of the experiences during this period are stored away in the unconscious portion of the mind. They may be revealed in later life through dreams or in psychotherapy.

The tiny ego thus begins its growth from the beginning of life. And if a child is satisfied in this period of sucking, feeding, and being held, a feeling of trust begins to grow within him. The contentment of being loved builds a person who will in turn be able to love other people. It is impossible to "spoil" a child in the nursing stage. He is not spoiled by nursing him when he is hungry and by cuddling and holding him to provide a sense of security. Babies who receive that kind of treatment usually need little else. They are calm and contented rather than frustrated and restless.

As we have seen, the first few months of an infant's life are centered around his physical nurturing, but if the baby is to grow into a receptive human, the nurturing must be done with loving attention. Socializing, in a limited form, begins very early in life. Some of the important early social experiences include eye contact while nursing and interaction with a smiling, cheerful mother who makes bathing and feeding times into opportunities for quiet, loving contact rather than times to perform necessary tasks in a hurry. The right attitude on the part of the mother helps the budding ego of the child to develop a feeling of deep security.

No psychosexual developmental stage ends at a precise time, and all of us retain a residue of infantile needs. If, however, our needs have been satisfied during each period of development, the infantile residue will be minimal. For instance, we all enjoy gratifying our oral feelings through eating, talking, kissing, and simply being aware of our mouths.

In all animals there is a natural biological urge to grow, but in humans there is also a psychological impulse to move on to an advanced stage of development. The impulse, however, needs to be encouraged and directed so that the oral child, for example, moves smoothly into the next stage of growth. If a mother is unable to wean her baby, it is probably because she enjoys the exclusive mutual arrangement with her baby so much that she unconsciously attempts to keep him dependent upon her.

A satisfied breast-fed child will eagerly begin to drink from a cup around eight or nine months and will wean himself by ten or eleven months. When he is tired, he may regress a bit by sucking his thumb and stroking a piece of cloth. These remind his unconscious mind of the pleasure of nursing, the thumb taking the place of the absent nipple, and the cloth serving to remind him of the breast skin he felt while nursing.

Bottle-fed babies seem to have a harder time giving up the bottle because it isn't as satisfying as the direct mother-child body relationship. They tend to cling to the bottle as if hoping to make up in some way for the lack of warmth.

In order to help the orally-oriented child move on to the next life stage, the mother must employ the gentle art of constructive frustration. After all, you cannot say to a child, "Well, now that's enough of your oral period; let's move on."

The mother can see and feel for herself when a baby

is ready to exert some self-control in life. After he has begun to walk, speak some words, and understand some of the words spoken to him, he is usually ready to enter the anal stage of life. The transition ordinarily occurs around fifteen to eighteen months of age.

He does not give up the oral pleasures entirely, but very gradually he stops sucking his food and learns instead to chew it. He begins to babble and then talk. If his ego has had a good beginning, he eagerly spends most of his waking hours relating to everyone and everything around him.

The oral stage of life is the only time when a person should be given unlimited love just because he is alive and in need of it. From then on in life, love must be earned. That is actually a fortunate characteristic of man, for it fosters self-esteem in the child to realize that he is capable of earning his way in the world.

If, through intuition and empathy with her infant, the mother gives sufficient attention to his needs, the child will be prepared to enter and pass through the anal period without excessive difficulty. Through her nurturing she will have implanted into his ego a feeling of trust. And he will need a strong sense of trust to help him face the task of growing up. The feeling of security that trust engenders will help him to develop and care for his own growing personality. A feeling of security is built by the fulfillment of his basic needs when he is completely helpless and dependent. In other words, the more love and care a mother gives her baby in the oral stage, the quicker he is able to advance in his subsequent psychological course.

When the baby emerges into the active life of the

crawler and toddler, he experiences a new sensation. That happens when he hears his first No! from his parent. He discovers that he can be a source of displeasure to this all-giving mother, and he begins to learn the facts about earning his way in the world.

Remember, he still has little control over his id impulses. He sees a bright object and his id directs him to have it *at once!* If he has received love, he has to make a decision when he hears his mother say "No." With his small resources he has to decide whether to follow his impulse, or, because his ego wants his mother's love, to forego the immediate pleasure of getting the bright object and thereby earn more love from his mother.

This is a drama which is acted out thousands of times from the beginning of the toddler stage until the child learns self-control. It is a necessary part of his psychological growth and the beginning of the development of his superego. The superego retains every No that the parents say to the child. Therefore, if he hears too many No's at this tender time of life, his natural capacities will become frozen and as an adult he will be unable to do much of anything on his own. On the other hand, if he hears too few No's he will develop a personality with defective controls and he will be unbearable to others.

Sometime during the second year, or between two and a half and three years of age, the child's sensuality slowly moves from the oral zone to the anal zone of his body. From the beginning of life the genital skin area has given the baby some passive pleasure. In her cleansing of the baby the mother mildly stimulates the genitals and anus. A normally sensualized being, he giggles and coos because he enjoys the sensations, but he is not keenly aware of his genital area. One reason he is not interested is because he cannot see it and cannot get it into his mouth the way he can his fingers, toes, toys, and all other available things.

When sphincter control becomes possible, around twenty-eight months, the sensual pleasure produced in this area is perceived by the child, and his psychic satisfaction is drawn away from oral gratification toward his anal zone. This is the time of toilet training, and the manner in which this period is handled profoundly affects the growing ego.

All children find their body by-products fascinating and important because they come from themselves. They are usually quite amazed that their parents find their feces smelly and unpleasant. They are also amazed that their parents want them to defecate into the toilet rather than in their pants. Second and third children seem to accept the idea of toilet training more readily because they see the older sibling casually giving up his body waste. But the first or only child has no peer to relate to, and often a struggle develops between his parents' wishes and his own.

Again we have the internal conflict of the id, ego, and superego. The id says, "It feels good to wet and dirty my pants." But the parent—and most often it is the mother—says, "If you want to earn my love, you must give up this body pleasure and be clean." If the child was loved during the oral stage, he wants to satisfy his parent's request and be loved, so he gradually learns to please her by using the toilet. After hearing praise from the parent, the superego lets the ego, or self, feel good and worthy of the parent's love.

Conversely, if the parent is too severe with the child, a struggle ensues that can affect all of the child's relationships. He will withhold his feces from the demanding parent because he feels rage at being pressed too hard. The result may be that throughout the remainder of his life his first response to any request made of him will be negative.

The healthy psychological residues of the anal period are a desire to be clean and neat, to have reasonable order in one's daily life, and to be willing to give of oneself.

You can see the important role that the mother plays through the oral and the anal stages of her child's development. Other family members are also perceived by the infant and they, too, affect the growth of his ego and superego, but to a considerably lesser degree.

Because the child's psychological apparatus is extremely frail, the parents must also protect the baby from external hostility. Just as they consciously save him from physical danger, they must not allow jealous siblings to bruise his young sense of self. If the parents allow an older brother or sister to harass the child during the late oral and the anal stages, the child's superego will gain excessive force and his ego will have to bear too much pressure.

During the anal period when the child continually tests the family for structure ("What can I do and not do?"), he must not be spoiled and allowed to indulge all of his still strong id desires. The healthy growth of his ego requires that he have a structure within which to operate, and he must learn what his permissible limits are within that structure. The discipline necessary to establish those limits need not consist of yelling or slapping.

Rather he should constantly be shown how to gain love by giving up his destructive id impulses. These aggressive drives are in all humans, but in the early stages of life they can be channeled into constructive avenues of expression. We must have constructive aggression in order to survive life. It is aggression that makes a baby cry to get his food, and it is aggression that compels him to test the parental structure when his superego begins to develop.

Therefore we should not try to squash the child's anal aggression by *forcing* him to stop wanting to break things, by demanding that he quit testing his limits, or even by forcing him to use the toilet. He needs that aggression, but if it is filtered through a strong ego, healthy self-esteem, and a fair and just superego, it can be used in the service of work and creativity.

A child in the anal stage would actually enjoy smearing his feces all over the place. The urge comes from his impulsive id. His mother, speaking for the superego, says that this cannot be done. She presents an option, an alternative form of conduct which, because it uses his ego as an ally, is acceptable to the child. The child is told that he can smear and make designs, but only with finger paints and only on the paper provided for him to use. He is told that he can make mud pies in the backyard or in a sandbox. The child thus learns that giving up the id pleasures can gain him substitute fun and approval. He can make things and at the same time gain praise and love for his young ego.

Mothers who do not allow children in the anal phase to play occasionally with dirty things, but who demand instead cleanliness at all times, thwart the natural aggression the child wants to express. The frustration the child feels causes a backup of anger in his id, and he becomes irritable. As a result, he may try to express his aggression by hitting and biting.

The parental job at this stage is very difficult because there is a delicate balance that must be established between giving a child what he wants and what he should have. His id wants everything: all the love, all the food, and all the attention. He needs *some* food, love when he deserves it, and attention to his changing person.

Boys and girls are much the same during the oral and anal periods of development. It is how they are handled by the mother figure that will determine how successfully they pass through those periods. People say that girls are easier to toilet-train than boys, but it is the manner in which the mother has related to the child as a person that determines whether the infant can relinquish his inclination to mess his pants.

You can see that from the beginning of life the stage is partially set for a child's personality. An infant is not a blank canvas at birth; he is an instinct-ridden, sensual being. And from the moment he is born he begins to learn about love and aggression. His parents mold his ego and superego over his seething instincts, and whether the whole ends up as a work of art or a confused, erratic construction largely depends on the mother.

The next stage of psychological growth is called the phallic stage. It is at this juncture of development that the male and the female differ radically. The phallic stage begins sometime in the third or fourth year of life. Again it should be noted that no child progresses evenly through the various stages of life but goes according to his own inner needs and his human environment.

I will first briefly explain the male's phallic stage so that the female's development can be contrasted with it. In the process of being toilet-trained during the anal period, the little boy has become increasingly aware of his penis. He derives sensual satisfaction from urinating, and his body structure dictates that he hold his penis in order to direct his urine flow into the toilet. The latter activity is also pleasurable, and he takes delight in his newly discovered instrument, directing his urine anywhere he pleases. Nature is getting the youngster ready for his sexual role in life by directing his attention toward his genitals.

New sensations begin to grow around the boy's penis and he feels additional pleasure in touching it even when he does not have to urinate. Active masturbation begins in the phallic stage although no ejaculation occurs. The child likes to fondle his body parts simply because it feels good. The same phenomenon is at work in this activity as when he derived enjoyment from sucking and learning to control his bowels.

Along with these new feelings, the little boy becomes aware of how deeply he loves his mother. Their relationship has always been significantly sensual, beginning at her breast. He does not consciously recall the breastfeeding, but his unconscious mind does. His mother also stimulated his feelings during the anal stage by cleaning him and by drawing his attention toward the anus by her request for cleanliness. Furthermore, she would have had to touch his penis in her bathing and diaper-changing chores. As you can see, therefore, the bond between mother and son is strongly sensual. Thus it is natural that when the boy's penis is stirred with new feelings of pleasure, he associates those sensations with his mother.

47

During the phallic stage the boy longs to have his mother completely for himself. This is the beginning of the Oedipal period. His id impulses, which are still stronger than his ego or superego, send out a demand, "I want Mom for myself! I hate everyone else who gets her love!" His father is thought of as a fierce competitor for the mother's affections. It is obvious to the boy that his mother and father have some kind of special relationship that does not include him.

An example of how a boy's conflict operates can be seen in James, a happy three-year-old. All day long he chatted with and helped his mother as she did the household chores. He followed her about with great love and attention. He was impatient when their daily routine was interrupted by the telephone or a visitor. Through his earlier stages of development, however, he had learned some patience and he was able to wait for his mother to return her attention to him.

But at six o'clock James changed from a cheerful, helpful little boy into an irritated and quite irritating child. The external event that caused this reversal of behavior was the daily homecoming of his father, the intruder. James was consumed with jealousy because his beloved mother happily welcomed her husband home from work.

Suddenly James did not like anything his mother had prepared for supper because he was angry with her for what he felt was an act of disloyalty. He began having a difficult time going to sleep because he wanted to sleep with his mother. In effect, he wanted to kick his father out into the night and take his father's place by his mother's side.

James's parents were aware of their son's turmoil and

began to help him move through what we now understand as the Oedipal period. Again, it is the mother's responsibility to gently frustrate the id wishes of her child so that he may grow. The father's role in this emotional maneuver is to be available when the boy is being "weaned" from the close mutual relationship with the mother.

James was encouraged to use his limited vocabulary to express his feelings. Through this method his parents taught him that his feelings were permissible to have and to talk about, but (and here enters the superego) it was not permissible for him to harm his father or take his place. By talking, and making up stories, and drawing pictures, James was able to ventilate a great deal of his natural anger toward both parents. In that way he worked off his hostility toward them for not giving him everything he wanted.

In the boy's Oedipal period he must eventually accept the fact that he cannot have his mother for his own. She belongs to his father. Sometime during the operation of his conflicting emotions it occurs to the boy that his father may be aware of his son's plans for the big take-over of the family. Since he has what amounts to murderous wishes toward his father, the child thinks that if his father finds out about them, he may harm him. The father, by reason of his size and authority, stands like a giant in relation to the child, a giant with great power. The boy's fear of harm becomes associated in his mind with his body's most sensualized precious part, his penis. The boy begins to fear that this giant, his father, will take away his penis. The fear does not develop because the child is aware of wanting to retain his penis in order to have intercourse, for he may not even know about genital contact. Because of his sexual development, however, his penis is his most important organ.

It is at this time that nightmares begin, usually with big bears or giants chasing the helpless little boy. It is also interesting to note that knives, which can cut off penises, are very prevalent in the lives of boys who are going through the Oedipal period.

If the parents are aware and helpful, however, the resolution of the Oedipal strivings can occur smoothly. By capitalizing on the child's admiration for his father's powers the father can gradually lead the boy to understand that if he wants a woman like his mother, he should identify himself with the father and that later he can go out into the world and seek a woman of his own. The wise mother undramatically draws away from the hitherto deep involvement with her son and lets the father lure him to his side.

This is a lengthy experience for the members of the triangle. It is replayed among them many times, just as in the anal stage the child relearns every day the structure and behavioral limits of the family.

The message given to the growing child's ego is, "If you renounce your id impulses toward your mother as the supergo directs, you will someday be a man like your father." This is the period, therefore, when gender identification is established in the child's ego.

The little boy must lose the Oedipal battle in order to become an independent person. Going away from home to begin school is an obvious symbol of his growing autonomy. If he has passed through his Oedipal period successfully, he will be able to use his psychic energy to learn academic skills. Children who have learning problems are usually those who are still embroiled in the Oedipal conflict and do not have enough energy to apply toward learning. That problem will be discussed in more detail in a later chapter when I describe the hang-ups that can occur during psychosexual development.

The female's phallic period is more complex than that of the male. In order for a girl to establish her female gender identity, she must go through two Oedipal periods. These periods may occur simultaneously or one may follow another. In either case the girl must go through two separate rejections and losses before she has resolved her Oedipal period of development.

As with the boy, the girl in the phallic period is concerned with her genitals and the new sensations she experiences. Because at the age of three her vagina is very tiny, her attention is drawn to her clitoris.

If you recall from Chapter II, the physical make-up of the clitoris is similar to that of the male penis and has the same capacity to give pleasurable sensations. Masturbation is just as pleasant for little girls as it is for boys.

Since the female infant begins life with the same life-sustaining relationship with the mother as the boy does, her new sensual feelings are also associated with the mother. Consequently she, too, has the id desire to have the mother as her exclusive property, and she suffers jealously when her father is perceived as an intruder into her highly sensualized bond with her mother.

Again the mother's role is to gently reject this insistent demand of the child and to direct her into a loving relationship with her father. The extent of the little girl's feeling of rejection depends upon the degree of ego strength she has already developed in the interactions of mother and daughter throughout the oral and anal stages.

Because nature has two sexes, the female's natural bent is toward heterosexuality and most females move eagerly from the Oedipal relationship with the mother into the Oedipal relationship with the father. If the two Oedipal struggles develop within the girl simultaneously, she then wants exclusive possession of the mother and of the father. And since they have a relationship with each other, she has love-hate feelings toward both of them at the same time. As you can imagine, such a period is filled with tremendous confusion and aggression for the child.

During the Oedipal attachment to her mother the female child may develop a wish to have a penis. The observant child sees that her father has a special relationship with her mother, and the child may reason that if she were a male like her father (which means having a penis), then perhaps she could gain all of her mother's affection. However, when the girl enters into the second Oedipal period, during which she exchanges the mother for the father in her quest for the prize, she becomes very "female" and relinquishes any desire she may have had for a penis. Having lost the first battle, the one for her mother, the child intensifies her efforts to win the second battle. She may even become overtly seductive with her father.

The father's role at this time is to respond to his daughter and convince her that she is indeed a very charming and delightful little girl—but she cannot take her mother's place. Because she has already been thwarted once, her ego must be handled with great gentleness in order for her to face the task of giving up the father as her exclusive love object. In effect, her father must send her back to the mother so that she can learn how to become a woman. He must persuade her that if she does this, she will learn how to attract a man of her own—a man like her father perhaps, but not him.

The female child must often feel like a Ping-Pong ball being batted back and forth between her feelings for her parents. She must be helped to resolve both of these emotional conflicts if she is to become a fully mature female being in her adult years.

The phallic stages of development are difficult to live through, and perhaps it is for that very reason that a quiet period occurs next. It is as if nature had decided that after throwing all that into a little child's existence in the first six years of life, the psyche should have a rest.

Between the ages of approximately seven and eleven years, most children live through a period of latent emotional development. If all the previous psychosexual development has been successful, the child's psychic energy is free to explore friendships outside the home and to acquire mastery of learning and physical skills. The child is able to engage in activities that feed his sense of self-esteem and help gain mastery over his aggressive impulses. His superego will have the opportunity to regulate his id impulses, and he will be able to love himself for appropriate reasons.

One may wonder why man has such an intense and aggressive id, but the reasons become clear when we consider the environmental conditions and problems that human beings had to face when they first appeared in the universe. Man was a roving animal whose role in life was to hunt and survive. His thinking, reasoning, and social abilities were minimal. Being a rather frail species by comparison with others, man needed an enormous amount of aggression in order to survive. Obviously nature's plan was successful, else the human race would now be extinct.

Evolutionary changes occur slowly, societal changes occur more rapidly. Our social order has evolved by leaps and bounds, whereas biologically and instinctually man at birth is not much different than he was in the beginning of his history. Just as women no longer need the abundance of eggs their bodies produce, neither do any human beings need all the aggression they are born with.

In order to manage all the instinctual aggression of the human being, society has to invent rules of behavior which become a vital part of each person's superego. We are born an aggressive, instinct-ridden being, and it is the parental job to build a strong ego and a just superego to cope with the powerful innate forces for survival that we inherit through our ancestry.

Among primitive man, the child beginning his physical growth spurt was required to take his place in an environment that was harsh and dangerous. Nature therefore provided the adolescent child with a great psychological push to complement his biological growth and enable him to be on his own. But society has changed radically and today's parents expect their children to continue to be dependent on them during their teen years. Yet the primitive adolescent forces are at work, and they come up against a changed social structure with a loud crunch!

Along with having to cope with physical growth, the

pubescent and adolescent child actually has to relive all his infantile psychosexual development. He has to attempt to master the oral, anal, phallic, and Oedipal stages for what is hopefully a final resolution. In addition, he is not as fortunate as the baby, who gets his stages sequentially. The adolescent is hit with all the developmental stages at one time.

Alleen had been an active youngster during her emotionally latent years, always athletic and talkative. Suddenly she becomes withdrawn and silent. She drops out of sports and loses interest in her friends and in school. She eats constantly, putting away enormous quantities of food. Right before dinner, she eats a huge "snack" of cookies, potato chips, and jelly doughnuts, and then, to her parents' amazement, she wolfs down her dinner. A half hour later, Alleen is in the kitchen again looking for something to eat.

She hates to wash her hair and seems to delight in wearing the oldest and dirtiest clothes she can find. She is secretive in all of her activities and demands a lock on the door of her room so "they" cannot invade her privacy. "They" stand for her brothers, sisters, parents, and other relatives.

Alleen is highly defensive and spends hours crying if anyone says a word against her current rock singer flame. She worries constantly about what might be a pimple developing on her nose, but if told that washing her face will help her complexion, she storms from the room in indignation.

She is always interrupting her parents' conversation, demanding attention, but will not speak when they set aside a more convenient time to talk with her.

She criticizes her mother's way of doing things, but is

an awkward, tearful failure when she attempts that same task. Although her mother is a very attractive woman, Alleen keeps trying to put her down by commenting unfavorably about her wrinkles and the "funny-looking veins" in her legs.

She can show unlimited sympathy for a stray cat, worrying about its health and tenderly feeding it, but she loses interest in it suddenly and for no apparent reason. She has no sympathy with her parents' feelings or plans. She has no interest in their jobs and activities. She has no patience with other family members. She is, in other words, consumed with herself.

Alleen is not a monster child, but a typical adolescent struggling with many internal biological and psychological phenomena. No wonder teen-agers are considered by most adults to be selfish and thoughtless. Nearly all the psychic energy of adolescents is occupied with basic feelings, and they have very little energy left for the high-level impulses of kindness, consideration, and thoughtfulness.

Most parents despair at the apparent loss of their carefree pre-pubescent child. They say they do not understand this new creature who is so suddenly changed in attitude and appearance from the child they were accustomed to.

Adolescence, however, must be looked upon as a time of reorganization and solidification of the person who was growing during childhood. For instance, Alleen's overeating is part of her struggle with the oral urge. Fortunately, adolescent physical growth is so active that oral indulgence does not usually lead to obesity.

The adolescent's preoccupation with avoiding bathing

and with wearing dirty clothes as a kind of badge is a manifestation of the anal period. But this behavior usually disappears when the adolescent becomes actively interested in a one-to-one relationship with a member of the opposite sex.

Many parents make a dangerous error during their child's adolescence. Because their own habits of eating and personal cleanliness are fixed, they assume that their child's preoccupation with junk food and a disordered appearance will continue forever. Demanding strict controls, however, simply activates the adolescent's old anal wish to oppose *any* request, and a struggle can begin that may last for years.

Granted it seems as if the teen-ager will always be a mess, but the less pressure used by the parents, the easier it will be for the adolescent to move on and change. Who wants to make a point of being dirty if no one will play the role of adversary?

Alleen's insistent need to interrupt her parents' relationship with each other is a replay of the Oedipal period. She wants to complain to her father about her mother and vice versa, hoping to gain the favored position. As in childhood, she wants to win all the love for herself. But if her parents were to allow themselves to become entangled in her Oedipal struggle, Alleen's growth process would be impeded.

Along with the resurgence of Oedipal feelings arrives the additional weight of adolescent turmoil. All the sensuality that is present in the infant arrives thundering upon the adolescent scene, but it is many times more intense in feeling. Nature's intention was that the adolescent should be on his own, defending life and limb and procreating, and indeed the adolescent's physical, emotional, and sexual growth was necessary to the preservation of primitive society. Such growth, however, is not suitable for today's world. Society has stipulated that during adolescence, when sexual feeling is at its height, the young person should be celibate. Thus another fierce dilemma is added to the oral appetite, the anal regression, and the phallic aggressive drive. It all seems too much to handle. In fact, it is too much for most adolescents to cope with, and that is why they desperately need understanding and tolerant parents to help them.

The young girl may dress in a provocative, sexy manner, almost defying her male teachers not to notice her curvy legs and budding bosom. She would, of course, be horrified if they actually made a pass at her because, although her body is ready for sexual intercourse, her emotions are not.

Masturbation is used to alleviate sexual tension, and along with masturbation go masturbatory thoughts. Fantasies of rape are common among female adolescents, because the young girl can rationalize, "I don't have any sexual desires, it's the man taking advantage of me." She may also have fantasies involving a romance with a forbidden and unreachable movie star or pop singer and of being a glamorous woman that all men grovel before.

Every part of the adolescent girl is sexualized, but at any given moment she may suddenly become the shy little girl who is all arms and legs and feeling "goofy." However, the eyes of most adolescent girls reveal their sexual feelings. Many of them refuse to look an adult squarely in the eyes for fear that the adult will comprehend their sexuality and scorn or punish them for those feelings.

Sometimes parents grow alarmed at the amount of aggression that the adolescent demonstrates. But the thing to remember is that the young person is pushed by instinctual id aggression, which is preparing him for the necessary break from his comfortable dependence on his parents.

Adolescent aggression must have at least a verbal outlet in the parental home. In order to be able to feel independent, the adolescent challenges the ideas and ideals of the parents. But his own ideas are not firmly established and his parents should not even assume that the opinions so vehemently held by their teen-ager will be the same the following week. In fact, he may take the opposite viewpoint and argue it with just as much vigor. Consequently, parents have to be flexible just at a time in their lives when their own patterns are becoming more rigid.

As in the childhood developmental stage, the adolescent's id aggressions deriving from the anal and phallic periods must be channeled into constructive means of expression. Sports are a particularly effective means of draining off some of the aggression. Physical work, creative activities, and intellectual competition can also provide constructive channels for expressing aggressive instincts. If, on the other hand, the adolescent is not allowed some expression of his individual differences, he will build up a dangerous backlog of aggression that may explode in physical aggression, drug use, or running away from home before he is fully equipped to deal with the world. The adolescent developmental process takes about as long as the first run-through of psychosexual development. Each day all the instinctual drives pound away at the twelve-to-eighteen-year-old ego structure, and youngsters going through the conflicts that these forces present must be handled with care by their parents. Thus, at a time in life when most parents are worn down from the responsibility of child rearing, this important test of their resources is made—the task of dealing with and helping the adolescent become an emotionally mature adult. It takes a great deal of energy.

It also takes a lot of love to enable parents to pay attention to and deal with the emotionally charged teen-ager. One day he seems adult and the next day he has regressed to the level of a jealous three-year-old child. The ego isn't strong enough yet to be entirely constant, but in the day-to-day mastery of id impulses the ego gradually gains strength.

If as a baby the teen-ager was given a good start in his ego development, then early unconscious feelings of love and trust are there to help him overcome his id wishes. But if the parents are unbending and demand constant adult behavior from the adolescent, the super-ego (which the parents represent) can crush the struggling ego. With his ego severely damaged or destroyed, the adolescent can develop either of two ways. He can completely give up his desire for independence and thus remain emotionally an infant the rest of his life, unable to form any but dependent relationships with others. Parents who do not understand this process may feel satisfaction in having a docile teen-ager, but the child's backlog of anger ultimately will be expressed in some other way. The result will be a dull, unproductive, and unloving adult. On the other hand, the adolescent who has had his ego destroyed can choose total rebellion, depending on whatever strength his ego has; in so doing he emotionally disowns his parents, but he still struggles with their powers the rest of his life by transferring feelings of hate to all authority figures.

Alleen's parents were loving people who liked peace and quiet and appreciated the serenity that had developed in their relationship over eighteen years of marriage. Both of them wished that Alleen could be sweet and happy, but they also knew that the reality was that they had a normal adolescent to help through life. They realized they would have to give up some of their peace and quiet in order to allow their daughter to become a woman.

Because they were aware of how easily adolescents regress to childish behavior when they are with their parents, they gave Alleen the opportunity to be away from them as often as she pleased. But they imposed one stipulation: that she keep up with her studies.

Imposing such a restriction was a way of using the ego's need to gain love to combat the id's desire for instant satisfaction. Alleen was intelligent and was told that if she worked as well as she could in school she would be able to go to her favorite camp for backpacking and ecology study.

They did not demand that Alleen make full use of her intellectual capabilities, knowing that a significant amount of her energy was employed in the adolescent struggle, but they did make it plain that they expected a reasonable application of her time and abilities. Instead of saying to her, "You must study for two hours every night," which would have had the effect of making Alleen feel like a child with no controls of her own, they asked her how much time she herself felt was necessary for her to spend in studying. They discussed, rather than demanded.

Recognizing Alleen's need to express her individuality, they allowed her to paint her room and put up posters and mementos on the walls in any way she liked. Of course, she was not just given a charge account to run wild with. The superego parental figure says to the child's ego, "Be yourself, but earn your own way." Alleen's id says, "Give it all to me for nothing." She was encouraged to verbally express her feelings of wanting to have everything free, but was also encouraged to understand the realities of life. The reality of expenses won out.

This encounter was a lesson to the adolescent ego structure. It learned that to express your creativity, you will do something on your own if you want strongly enough to accomplish it. For example, Alleen baby-sat and tutored younger students to get the money for her decorating spree. When she had earned the money she needed, she painted her room a deep purple with pink and black "splotches" and put up various colorful decorations. She thought it was "absolutely fantastic" and brought in crowds of friends to share her admiration of the room.

Her parents admittedly felt queasy whenever they looked at the colors, but they kept to their resolve not to interfere with her choice. With their mature perspective, they realized that the room was Alleen's "personal space in life." From a practical point of view, it was only one room in their house and Alleen, after all, was living in it.

Decorating such as Alleen had done was typical of the adolescent need to say, "I'm different from you, and that difference makes me feel like an individual person." It is a productive form of self-expression. Incidentally, it commonly happens that the more bizarre the decoration scheme, the more quickly the adolescent tires of it and wants to adopt something more in harmony with the rest of the house.

As understanding as parents such as Alleen's are, the female's complicated Oedipal structure still causes the adolescent girl to be supersensitive to rejection. Because her unconscious memory bank urges repetition of her past history, she continually sets up emotional situations in which she feels rejected by both parents. Alert parents are aware of this repetition need and try to mitigate the adolescent girl's feelings of rejection. Nonetheless, the teen-ager will inevitably suffer some feelings of rejection.

Teen-agers need frequent periods of privacy, because they have an extremely active fantasy life. Their fantasies arise from their id instincts and may variously be romantic and heroic or aggressive and hostile. The thing to remember is that fantasies are only images with feelings, not actual deeds. For example, a child or adolescent may drift into thoughts of burning down the house with his parents trapped inside. The usual adolescent will feel guilt coming from the superego for having such a murderous id fantasy. When children feel guilty, they seek punishment to relieve the unpleasant anxiety state it creates. Therefore, he might follow such a fantasy with some act that would demand punishment, such as going into the kitchen and devouring the cold roast beef that had been planned for supper. His parents can then punish his selfish behavior, and thereby alleviate his guilt. However, that still leaves the aggressive phallic feelings untouched, unexplained, and still seething.

Parents should not be shocked that their daughter may at times have angry and hateful feelings toward them. Rather she should be encouraged to talk about her feelings, both the positive and the negative, but especially the negative. If she is allowed to ventilate her negative emotions verbally, they will fade away within a reasonable period of time. But if no expression is permitted, the emotions will continue to seethe in her unconscious. Eventually they will find an expression, usually in self-destructive behavior. That is why so many teen-agers are accident-prone. It is their own unspoken aggression toward the parents, turned back on themselves and their own bodies.

The same mechanism operates with reference to other guilt-producing behavior. For example, an adolescent may continually perform an irritating habit, such as nail-biting, hair-twisting, or slouching, in order to center the parents' anger on that behavior rather than on some masturbating fantasy or activity he feels guilty about.

Clearly it is not material wealth and possessions that enable an adolescent to develop into a mature person. The adolescent needs most what money cannot buy— a great deal of understanding, guidance, and unselfish love. Even with all of that, the adolescent girl will go through many trials and make many errors. But if handled properly, she will gradually master again her instinctual drives of orality, anality, phallic aggression, and her Oedipal conflicts.

The final resolution of this process comes when she can leave home prepared mentally as well as physically for the effort of establishing herself as an individual person in the world. Making that effort takes great emotional energy, and the young adult needs to be free of adolescent "hang-ups" in order to live fully. If she has been allowed to develop independence, she will be able to rely on her own judgment when decisions have to be made. She will be able to do so because she has sufficient self-esteem (ego strength) and because her superego will be reasonable and just.

Because she has had love and care from her mother and father she will be able to feel and express loving and sharing feelings with other people who are worthy of them. Friendships, therefore, will be based on mutuality of respect, love, and fairness.

Her sexual feelings will be a natural part of her personality, and ultimately she will be able to transfer the deep love feelings for her father to a man of her own choice. In the mature person there is a need to find another soul to join with in a mutually satisfying relationship. There is the wish to depend on and to be dependable, to take care of and to be taken care of with dignity, not as a child craves but as an adult who gives and receives from a position of confidence and self-esteem.

Because of the delicate structure of the female's psychosexual development, it is rare to find a woman who is truly emotionally mature. Many errors are made by parents which destroy or impede the female's natural developmental process. Therefore, in the next chapter, I will explore the problems that can arise in the young girl's personality during her developmental stages.

IV.

PROBLEMS
ALONG THE WAY

The primary goal in life is to grow to emotional maturity. Psychoanalysts speak of the emotionally mature person as one who has a "genital" personality. Contrary to the popular misconception, this term does not refer to people whose lives and interests are centered on sex but rather to those who have successfully traveled through and resolved the conflicts of all the phases of their psychosexual development. Or, to put it more specifically, the genital character is the final stage of the adult personality and represents a synthesis of the earlier oral, anal, phallic, and Oedipal stages as modified by social demands.

Margaret had not reached genitality. She was an alcoholic who had begun drinking at the age of sixteen and continued for the next fifteen years. At the age of thirty-one she still lived with her parents, even though she constantly quarreled with them and the home situation was generally unpleasant. She was unable to hold a job for more than a month. Although she could pull herself together to pass interviews and be accepted for employment, her absenteeism started in the first week. When she did go to her job, she was usually hung over and unable to carry out her work competently. She was caught in a vicious cycle. No one, she felt, would give her a chance, so she sought further solace in drinking, which of course only compounded her difficulties.

Her parents were nondrinkers and would not allow liquor in the house. It was there, however, hidden away in the various ingenious hiding places Margaret had devised over the years.

To be able to get the liquor she needed, Margaret resorted to a number of devices. She stole money from her parents when she could, and on one occasion she took money from the purse of a visitor. She made it a practice to sit around in bars and let herself be picked up in exchange for drinks. Often she woke up in a strange bed with a man she could not even remember meeting. If these strangers gave her money or offered her a bottle, she would cooperate in any act they requested or demanded.

Margaret was, to put it bluntly, a mess. She drifted through her shabby life in an alcoholic stupor. She actually felt some sensation of pleasure only with the first two or three drinks. After those few, she in a sense mentally passed out, although she seemed to be aware of what she was doing. Her main goal in life, her reason for living, was to get that next drink.

As gruesome as this picture is, Margaret was not an unusual case. She was typical of the millions of Americans who suffer from alcoholism. True, there are many drunks who are more functional than Margaret. They hold jobs, act as fathers or mothers and marriage partners. But they all have the same type of mental disorder —they really do not care much about anything else but sucking on that bottle. They usually feel great self-pity, and they suffer from acute loneliness because they cannot sustain any deep interpersonal relationships in life. It is impossible to relate to other people when you are consumed with an overwhelming desire to drink.

What has happened to these people? What has caused them to keep bumping along in a groggy, unending search for an impossible utopia? The answer is that alcoholics are prime examples of people stuck in the oral stage of psychosexual development.

Remember, it is a stage of *id-ness* which seeks only self-satisfaction and does not include consideration of or thoughts about other people except to the extent that other people can be used to satisfy the oral cravings.

Margaret's parents did nothing to help her. Despite the evidence before them, they denied to themselves that their daughter was a very sick person. They maintained the hope that someday she would meet a nice man and, by some miracle, straighten out and stop having problems. What they themselves were unwilling to do, they expected someone else to do for them. Through their passive silence and denial of reality they effectively encouraged her to continue drinking.

She came to me for consultation after being referred by a woman who had interviewed her for a job. The interviewer herself was a reformed alcoholic who spotted Margaret's problems immediately and suggested to her that if she wanted a job, she would have to seek some kind of treatment.

Treatment is not easy for either the alcoholic patient

or for the psychoanalyst. An alcoholic has very little ego or superego to work with. As you recall, the ego grows primarily during the oral stage, the superego during the anal stage. A person who ceases to grow beyond the oral stage is still infantile. He cannot tolerate the frustration that analysis frequently creates.

To start with, I asked Margaret to tell me her life story. It was, indeed, a sad one.

When she was born, her father was out of the country doing Red Cross work. He was admired by his colleagues for his dedication to his work, but in reality he was running away from his wife and family. He supported them financially but was an emotionally absent husband and father.

Margaret was the third child and had not been wanted by either parent. Those were the years before legal abortions and before women were free enough to admit to themselves that they didn't always want a baby. Her two sisters, who were two and four at the time of Margaret's birth, were themselves neglected youngsters. They quite naturally looked upon the new arrival as an enemy who would steal away the meager attention they were getting from their depressed mother.

Margaret remembered that when she was older her mother used to complain bitterly to her about what a nuisance she was as a baby. She described how Margaret would cry and scream all day and night. "You were a horrible baby!" she said. "And the only time you shut up was when I popped a bottle in your mouth and left you in your crib."

Margaret obviously received none of the nurturing experience so necessary for an infant during the oral period. She was not even held for her feeding but was fed by a propped-up bottle. No one in the family cared for her needs. She remembered being very shy and frightened as a young child and trying to cling to her mother's skirts. "She always pushed me away and scolded me," Margaret recalled.

As a result of her fears and insecurity, Margaret spent a lot of time crying and sucking her thumb. School was a blur of confusion. Her main memory of those years was of trying to concentrate while biting her nails. Biting her nails was an act of pleasure for her.

Her father came home when she was four, but he was silent and withdrawn. As often as possible he was away from the house.

Margaret started going out with boys when she was thirteen, but as time went on, she found it difficult to keep a boyfriend. One boy bluntly told her that she was too demanding—she wanted to be held, kissed, and taken out, but she did not show any interest in him in return. He felt as if he were simply being used by her.

As she continued to grow and develop, Margaret continued to be clinging and jealous—unappealing qualities in anyone. Everywhere she went, she quickly got herself rejected.

In the unconscious part of everyone's psychological make-up are stored all the things that are done to or for him. Before thought and conscious memory develop, the unconscious memory bank begins to build its storehouse of personal experiences. As one grows older, his unconscious wants to repeat what it is already familiar with. So the unconscious pushes the individual to play the original scenes over and over again. Thus, if you come from a happy family situation filled with mutual love and affection, the unconscious part of your mind will seek out people similar to your parents with whom you can experience life. This mechanism is called the "repetition compulsion." It operates in everyone.

From the very beginning of her life Margaret's experiences primarily involved withholding and rejection. Consciously she wanted to love herself and someone else, but in her unconscious there was a different program. What she really longed to do was impossible, because the repetition compulsion led her to act in such a way that people continually rejected her just as she had been rejected in her infancy. As an adult, she was as frustrated by the world as she had been as a baby.

She therefore returned to the only minor satisfaction she had ever had in life—oral pleasures experienced alone. Just as she had had her bottle as a baby, so had she "progressed" to sucking her thumb and biting her nails, until finally at a party during high school she discovered liquor.

Her unconscious pattern was to attempt things in a tentative manner and then to sabotage her opportunity. The pattern was the same in nearly all situations, whether it was meeting a new person, taking a job, or dating a man. She behaved in this way because her ego had never developed enough to give her the strength to either try hard or attempt options. Having never gone beyond the oral stage, she acted in a way that was reminiscent of her bottle-feeding days. Her behavior insured that she would repeat her early feelings of rejection, and she took to the bottle for solace. Instead of the warm milk given to her as an infant, however, she substituted liquor. But the satisfaction was the same, the sensation of warm liquid in her mouth and traveling down her throat.

Sitting in my office, then, was an orally frustrated and deprived woman who had been seeking mothering all of her life. I recommended Alcoholics Anonymous for her, because that group gives mothering in a special way. The members admit to themselves and to each other that they are sick. They join together in a large familylike unit and demonstrate gentle care and concern for one another. They socialize as a group, and each is always available to help the others. By providing this unselfish maternal attention to the new member, they help the oral character to begin the ego growth that had been stunted.

The members of AA acknowledge that they are all lost in their id instincts (although they do not necessarily use that term) and have the need to get "milk" (alcohol) by sucking on a bottle. So they band together and give mothering which makes them feel loved and cared for and promotes ego growth. Most important, the alcoholic feels there is something to gain by relinquishing the infantile need to suck. Overcoming that need means getting praise from the group, approval from the group superego.

The AA system works because it gives its members a new chance in life based on family feelings of understanding and love. Psychotherapy is no substitute for that type of relationship.

Margaret reported to me a year later. She had kept her job, and most of her time was spent with other AA members. She admitted that she had slipped back to the bottle several times when she had suffered minor rejections. However, she was gradually feeling stronger as a person and was learning to be able to love. Now she is helping other people who are afraid they will resume drinking. When necessary, she gets up at night to go and stay with another frightened person. She can perform such an act of generosity because it was done for her.

Margaret is realistic in appraising herself. She feels that she has a long way to go yet, and she is right. She has started on the way, though, and the mothering experience she has received through AA has helped her to begin life again. She knows that she will be able to benefit from psychotherapy when she has conquered her compulsive oral needs. By that time she will have developed ego and superego structures and thus have the necessary psychological tools with which to work.

Just as a child can become lodged in the oral stage through deprivation, so too can the child who is overindulged. A mother impedes emotional growth if she allows her child to continue nursing or sucking on a bottle past the normal time of weaning. What she is doing is seducing the child's unconscious into believing that oral pleasures are the best thing in life. That is what causes obesity. The fat person's unconscious has been taught that eating is better than being slim and healthy, better than having a good sex life and loving and being loved.

Mothers who use food as a reward ("If you're good, you'll get dessert!") are implanting the notion into the child's unconscious that food means love. Food is not love. Food is nourishment that is needed to fuel the body. If a mother consciously or unconsciously seeks to keep her child dependent and close to her, she can use food as a weapon against the child's development. She can develop a pattern of giving her toddler food to soothe his bumps, scrapes, and other discomforts. As a result the child, both then and in the future, will always seek food when faced with any kind of trouble.

Again you can see the importance of the mother's role in the child's life. The importance of giving in the right direction and the responsibility of frustrating the id impulses of the child to foster growth cannot be underestimated.

Some mothers truly enjoy their infants during the oral stage and do an excellent job of mothering, giving their babies good starts in ego development. Many, however, fail in the next stage.

Jennifer's mother was an example of that type of woman. She happily cared for Jennifer when she was an infant because she liked being in control of the child. However, when Jennifer began to walk, to explore her surroundings, and in general to assert herself as a separate individual, her mother felt that her position of dominance was threatened. A struggle thus began between mother and daughter that was to last for many years.

The mother, for instance, insisted on Jennifer's being clean at all times. She talked constantly to the child about germs and dirt and painted a grim picture of what happened when germs invaded the body. She made the little girl sit for hours on the toilet, demanding that she get into the habit of moving her bowels at exactly the same time every morning. Naturally Jennifer's ego rebelled against such treatment. She would cry and plead with her mother to let her get up, but her mother remained adamant. As a result Jennifer withheld her feces until she was napping. Then, when she was in a relaxed state, her body would expel the feces. That, of course, made her mother even more angry, and the battle continued for several months until finally Jennifer gave in.

It was not just in the bathroom that the power game was played, but in every area of Jennifer's life. From that time on, her mother sought ways in which to manipulate her. She chose the child's playmates and would not allow her to play with any "messy" children. She not only selected all of her daughters clothes but each day laid out what she was to wear. She even interfered when Jennifer was playing a game or coloring and told her how she was to do things.

As a result of all this, Jennifer appeared to be a quiet, mousy child who was too frightened to speak up for herself. Some family friends considered her a "model" child. But in Jennifer's unconscious the anger and rage against her mother was growing daily.

Jennifer's father was no ally because he too was completely dominated. Even though he was an adult, his relationship to his wife was similar to Jennifer's relationship with her.

Because Jennifer was never allowed to make any decisions, she was at a complete loss when she entered the social world of school. It was not until adolescence, when she was no longer helpless, that the stored-up aggression of fifteen years burst forth.

In this new phase of behavior Jennifer would do nothing positive that was demanded of her. That was a shock to her mother, for over the years she had become comfortable in her role as dictator over her family. She had always been in control and expected to continue her strong influence on her daughter's life for as long as she lived, just as she had always dominated Jennifer's father. She had even planned for the kind of man whom Jennifer would marry and the number of grandchildren she expected the couple to produce.

Normal adolescent aggression is difficult enough for the average parent to deal with, but when there is so much pent-up anger, it is even more difficult. The anal rage-aggression that exploded in Jennifer was fired with years of holding back. She would not bathe or wash her hair for weeks at a time. She yelled defiance at her shocked parents and refused to buckle under her mother's discipline again—"not ever again!" were her words. Physical blows were exchanged between mother and daughter. Yet these things did little to relieve Jennifer's feelings—instead, her rage burned with even more intensity. Eventually there was the predictable outcome— Jennifer went into complete rebellion and ran away from home. She has never returned.

What caused this so-called "nice" child to become so angry that she took such a final step? In her unconscious Jennifer had learned to be controlled only by an external force. She had not been given the opportunity to control herself. She transferred her hate of her controlling mother and her passive, ineffectual father to the world at large. Nearly every person with whom she came into contact became her enemy. She felt that everyone wanted to control her in some way, so she was hostile to whomever she met. Her idea was to fend them off by hostility before they could get a chance to overpower her.

There were no gray areas in her approach to life, no compromises. To her mind it was either control or be controlled. She was stuck in her anality and viewed the world as a struggle for power.

Because it is possible for a young person to run away and never be found, Jennifer fared well for herself after she left home. She roamed the countryside, "crashing" at known hip places and stealing food or leeching from various communes. She eventually ended up with a group of revolutionists who were trying to disrupt a university.

Jennifer's new friends all hated anyone in a position of authority. They spent their time planning and carrying out acts of violence.

Jennifer feels angry *all* of the time, from the moment she wakes until she falls into a restless sleep at night. She is a loner who cannot love. She thinks that love is just another means of controlling another person. In her words, "People who are stupid enough to fall in love are just asking for it!"

Every time she throws a rock or shrieks obscenities at a policeman, she is unconsciously retaliating for the treatment her mother gave her. Emotionally she is still a three-year-old child. However, she has the powers of an adult body which permit her to act out her murderous id instincts on the world. She has no superego to curb her aggression. In a sense she has never really left home because she relates emotionally to the world as if it were her mother trying to control her.

Just as in the oral stage deprivation and overindulgence can lead to emotional problems later in life, so too can those extremes in the anal stage.

Jennifer's case illustrates the results of excessive control. But if a child receives no control from his parents, if he is not toilet-trained at all, if he is allowed to be destructive of property and generally out of control, the result will be disastrous. The child who is given no external control will not develop an internal sense of self-control.

The symptoms of anal personalities are numerous and are extremely common in our society. They include such traits as always being late for appointments and not being able to maintain a schedule. These seemingly innocent everyday phenomena can be examined with our psychoanalytic knowledge of the anal period.

Any time two people arrange a meeting or appointment there is an unspoken, mutual agreement that they will be prompt. Each one is asking and expecting something of the other. The genital person responds and arrives on time because it is part of his or her character structure to be thoughtful. The genital person has an orderly life and does not waste either his time or another person's time. The anal personality, however, unconsciously resents having to do anyone else's bidding, even when it is to his own advantage. In fact the anal personality feels angry at being requested to be someplace at a certain time. But he cannot show his anger directly, because that would expose his infantility, so instead he withholds himself from his friend and is late. What he does is to make his friend as angry as he himself unconsciously is. The anal person in such a case appears to be innocent of any conscious wrongdoing. Anal people always have a variety of seemingly legitimate reasons for their tardiness, but those reasons are cover-ups for unconscious motivations. As patients, for example, they will be just five minutes late for every appointment.

Procrastination, difficulty in making even minor decisions, miserliness, slowness of speech, and the inability to wake up in the morning are all symptoms which develop in the anal period and become full-blown in adulthood. They are symbolic fecal mechanisms of withholding time, withholding words and ideas, withholding the self from the rest of the world. The anal personality is still protesting as if the world were the demanding parent who says, "Give up your waste material!"

If your first inner response is No when you are asked to do a task, to answer a question, to keep an appointment, or to make a decision, you have residual negative symptoms of the anal period. The same is true if you find that quick people confuse you with their alertness, or if you *must* maintain an antiseptically clean house or its opposite, a disorderly, unclean house. These negative characterisitics seriously interfere with living a full life.

Thus the fine line between positive and negative child-rearing makes itself more apparent as we examine further oral and anal periods of personality development. Similar symptomatology appears if a child is given too little or too much in regard to his emotional needs. Another condition that can result from either parental error is called narcissism.

Every person begins life with primary narcissism, the total emotional investment in oneself. Infants need to be narcissistic in order to survive. They have to cry out their demands for food, warmth, and care. If the infant is cared for and loved, he will be able to take that energy source of self-love and direct it toward others as he grows older. If a child is deprived emotionally in the oral stage, or kept in the sucking stage too long, his primary narcissism remains. In addition, if during the anal phase a child is not taught self-control, or if he is treated in an overly strict and repressive manner, the same condition prevails. The primary narcissism remains and grows inward. Hence that person can visualize the world only through his own self-love.

Narcissistic people are unable to love or feel empathy for others because all of their feelings are still trapped in themselves. Everything about the narcissistic character is inordinately precious—to himself. Narcissistic people can only maintain relationships that are based on mutual admiration for themselves.

If narcissistic individuals cannot get other people to admire and applaud their life, beauty, gifts, and talents (even when they have very little to offer), they boast, brag, and in general exaggerate their worth. If a mother is overindulgent and sees everything that her daughter does as "just marvelous," then she encourages the little girl to think of herself as a "princess." Alas, the real world is quite a shock to this unprepared child, especially when she reaches adulthood.

Most people see themselves with enough reality to realize and know that there is little room for royalty in this world. Moreover, love lavished exclusively on the self is wasted because it does not result in the joy of sharing that is essential to a full, mature life.

The difference between healthy self-esteem and narcissism is that self-esteem begins its growth through loving nurturing in the oral stage. During the anal period the individual learns to earn self-esteem by giving up instinctual pleasure for praise from the parents.

Ego esteem grows throughout life whenever the outer-oriented person does something worthwhile, whether it be a simple act of kindness or earning a college degree. Self-esteem is lowered in such an individual if he goes against his fair superego and allows his id instincts to have their way.

The narcissistic personality feels that he deserves acclaim just for existing. He feels no need to work for good relationships, jobs, or rewards, because he feels that they should come to him as a matter of course. It takes a great deal of denial of reality to maintain this narcissistic level of living, because beyond parental adulation the world is rather stingy with praise.

If a child is exceptionally beautiful and grows up to be a gorgeous woman, she can readily find a man who will adore her. However, surface beauty fades in all humans and the narcissistic person usually becomes deeply depressed when this state of life is reached.

It is a sorrowful thing to be either overindulged or deprived so as not to be allowed to grow beyond self-love.

During the phallic and Oedipal periods more problems can arise, although they are simpler to treat because they are farther along in the psychosexual development. In addition, this phase occurs at the time of speech and thought development and is thus available to conscious memory. That is, it is available to most people's conscious memories, especially among those who are highly motivated to change and grow.

"Call me Bill," boomed a woman in her late twenties who had come to see me because of a recurring symptom. She wore her hair closely cropped, and she even affected sideburns. Her suit was obviously purchased at a boys' clothing store. She swaggered as she walked into the office.

"I'm pretty damned embarrassed at coming to see a shrink, but my wife insisted I get this crazy itch cleared up. It drives her buggy, and she's a sensitive soul—not tough like me!"

So much bravado! Bill was trying to let me know that she was a "butch" Lesbian and not the least interested in hiding the fact.

She described her problem as being "inconvenient," as she had an overwhelming desire to scratch her crotch, particularly when she and her "wife" were out in a social gathering. Bill laughed about the problem openly, but her nervous girlfriend found it vulgar and embarrassing.

I explained to Bill that in order for us to understand this itching urge, it would be helpful to go back into her past and see if we could find clues to her problems.

"Now don't fool around with my 'Les' trip," she informed me. "I'm happy and I don't want anything to change. I should have been a man, you know, but things didn't work out that way. So I make it work out for me. My little wife, Susie, is all I have in the world, so don't mess with me there."

That was not a shocking statement to me, as most

homosexual people have little motivation for change. In our modern, sophisticated society, they are no longer looked upon as outcasts. My job as a psychoanalyst is to attempt to help people to love, work, and be creative to the best of their capabilities. If a patient is willing to do his or her part, then I must respond by doing my work to my fullest capabilities. I am neither a god nor magician, and I have to take into consideration my patient's desires. If Bill wanted only to stop itching, I promised that I would do everything I could to help her. I also advised her, however, that in the course of our work together I could not guarantee that she would continue to be a Lesbian—I was an analyst, not a fortune-teller.

Bill told me her background. Her real name was Wilhelmina. She was an only child, and her mother had lavished attention on her every move. She took weekly photographs to show Wilhelmina's progress and kept this up until Wilhelmina was seventeen years old. The pictures were lovingly placed in a ten-volume album set that was still cherished by her mother.

Wilhelmina's father had a different view of his only child. He had been a semifamous athlete in his youth and longed for a boy he could play ball with and teach the so-called manly arts, a son who would carry on the athletic tradition. He was deeply disappointed at the birth of a girl and showed no interest in her growth or emotional development.

An emotionally mature mother would have sought a change in her husband's behavior. Instead Wilhelmina's mother withdrew her affections and interest from her husband and placed them onto her little girl. As if to spite him, she made a point of dressing little Wilhelmina in frilly and dainty clothes. She saved every piece of paper that Wilhelmina scribbled on and made scrapbooks of all her school papers. In her mother's heart Wilhelmina was the star of the show and the center of the universe. Nothing was too good for her little girl.

Since she knew no normal frustrations, by the age of three Wilhelmina was an eternal optimist. Everything in her life was perfect for her, and she knew of nothing else, no opposition. It was natural, of course, for her ego to expect that life would always be so smooth and bountiful.

When she began to experience her Oedipal feelings for her mother, her withdrawn father was little competition. She told me that one day when she saw her father pushing his "big, ugly" body up against her mother while she was doing the dishes, she felt overwhelmed by rage. She promptly bit her father on his leg and as he was about to discipline her, her mother stepped between them, defending her "baby." Enraged, the father raised his hand to strike his wife. Seeing that, Wilhelmina bit him again, and then she and her mother ran to a neighbor's house to get away from what her mother called "that awful brute."

It was only a short while after this that Wilhelmina balked at wearing frilly clothes, refused to wear anything but blue jeans, and insisted on being called "Willy." Though distressed by this turn of events, her mother did not change her pattern of giving in to her daughter's every wish. She acceded to all of "Willy's" demands, and they continued their happy relationship.

If you recall, in normal psychosexual development

these intense feelings of ownership of the mother are normal in little girls. It is the mother's role, however, to gently frustrate her daughter's desires so the girl can repress them and transfer those love feelings to her father. And it is the father's role to lure the girl away from her infantile attachment to the mother. These are the years of gender identification in which parents must instill the sense of femaleness in the girl.

Wilhelmina's mother had no desire to give up her exclusive relationship with her daughter. She had always treated Wilhelmina as an extension of herself, lavishing all the attention on her daughter that she herself had wanted as a child.

By excluding the father who was, it is true, a willing absentee emotional factor, Wilhelmina's mother stopped the child from growing. Wilhelmina became arrested in her first Oedipal period and in effect became a "little husband" for her mother. In her costume of pants, with her dominating, bossy behavior and her contempt for her father, she really was the man of the house. She resented her father's sexualized hug of her mother and unconsciously identified with him in order to take his place.

On one occasion when her mother became ill and was hospitalized, Willy was left with her father and a babysitter. The sitter was unable to stay after supper, and it was left to Wilhelmina's father to care for her in the evening. She remembered that on that first evening they were alone, she felt an unaccustomed warmth toward him and went over and sat beside him on the sofa as he watched the news on television. She felt lonely and affectionate, so she leaned over and kissed his cheek. But after all these years of disinterest in her and anger over the secretive relationship between his wife and daughter, he was in no mood to show affection to "the brat" as he called her. Instead of responding kindly to her gesture, he pushed her away and told her to go to her room.

Thus Wilhelmina's instinctual but hesitant push to be heterosexual was abruptly snuffed out. She was crushed by her father's rejection. She never again made such a gesture, nor did she go out of her way to speak to him. When he died in her twentieth year, she refused to attend his funeral.

From the time of her father's overt rejection, Wilhelmina maintained the first Oedipal attachment to her mother and became more and more of a little man. Her fantasies were of winning great glory as an Olympic athlete and coming home to present her medals to her mother. Throughout grammar school, life was easy for her, because if she had any problems, her mother fixed things and found solutions for her. Her mother even insisted that the teachers call her daughter Willy rather than Wilhelmina.

During Wilhelmina's puberty and adolescence, her mother made sure there were outlets for her daughter's malelike aggression, and Wilhelmina played every rough game that was available. But Wilhelmina had one problem her mother could not solve for her—menstruation. Wilhelmina told me that she was very upset when she began menstruating. She said it disgusted her and she thought it was a sign of weakness to bleed like a "stupid girl" every month. In addition, she suffered from such severe cramps that her menstrual periods were almost unbearable.

Wilhelmina's cramps were a body reaction against

being female. She did not want to be a woman, so her unconscious provided evidence to prove she was right in preferring to be a man. In effect, it said to her—see how painful and gruesome menstruation (i.e., womanhood) is. Her mother placated her with the promise that when she got older she could have all those things taken out that were causing the bleeding.

So Willy went swaggering through her life. She felt good and strong and very pleased with her world and her physical achievements. And always at her side was her mother who was eager to tell her what a real pal and helpmate she was.

When Willy was twenty-one she met a girl through mutual friends. Susie, like Willy's mother, thought that Willy was just the greatest person in the world. Having never grown up, Susie was an infantile who was looking for someone (anyone) on whom she could be dependent. She made Willy feel very masterful, and flattered and adored her in much the same manner as Willy's mother had always done. Willy and Susie set up housekeeping and called themselves husband and wife. Soon Willy changed her name to Bill.

Wilhelmina's mother was furious that her daughter would leave home, as she expected their unconscious marriage to last a lifetime. She begged, pleaded, and threatened, but Wilhelmina was adamant about living her new life. The emotional four-year-old that was the basis of Wilhelmina's personality structure wanted to be with her new, adoring, and more appealing mate.

The itch appeared whenever Bill and Susie were in mixed company. Bill admitted that when she was around men she would suddenly feel uncomfortable and jealous of them. She would find herself staring at men's crotches to "catch a glimpse." Then her crotch itch would develop. She said she felt gleeful at the embarrassment of the men present as she openly scratched herself.

I suggested to Bill that she was acting out a feeling of not really being a man because she had no male genitals. In effect, by "scratching her balls," as she called it, she was pretending she did have them. Bill's reaction to my interpretation was an astounded "I'll be damned!" She then decided that the best thing to do was to avoid all men and thus get rid of the itch.

That kind of simplistic solution is typical of a four-year-old who denies all unpleasant experiences and avoids them in the future. Bill never returned for further treatment but sent a note thanking me for "shrinking away the itch—Ha-ha!" She added, somewhat defensively I thought, that she "and the little woman were really having a *ball*."

Many people are quite offended by homosexuality, which is not a realistic attitude. Homosexuality is just another symptom of a lack of progress in psychosexual development. Obesity is not looked upon with horror by most people, nor is obsessive behavior. The reason so many women feel offended by female homosexuality is that they have had to repress their own homosexual feelings and renounce the very wishes and actions that Lesbians carry out.

All females begin life in a homosexual relationship with the mother. In order to gain genital maturity, those strivings to own the mother must be replaced with love for the main male figure in a girl's life. It is a difficult emotional experience to move away from the life-sustaining mother into the unknown territory of the male-female world. Women who react violently against Lesbians are usually trying to deny their own homofilial feelings. Feelings of love for another woman, however, are quite normal and enjoyable to the genital female. She accepts those feelings as natural and recognizes that they can be the basis for many rich and enjoyable friendships between women.

There are many factors involved in homosexuality. A possessive, indulgent mother can be one cause but there are others. Sometimes when a little girl becomes attached to and seductive with her father, the father is unable to handle the situation correctly. If that happens, he can cause his daughter to regress emotionally to her first Oedipal longings for the mother.

On the other hand, a father who feels aroused by his miniature woman-daughter may think himself evil for having what actually is a normal reaction to the child. Acting on his self-condemnation, however, he may completely withdraw from his daughter's life, thereby rejecting her. Or he may project his feelings about himself onto his daughter, regarding her as naughty and "dirty" for arousing sexual feelings within himself for her—a forbidden object of sexuality. Instead of understanding and accepting his feelings as a normal part of love between an emotionally healthy father and daughter, he becomes angry with his child and rejects her. However the rejection is manifested, it occurs at a time when the child needs her father most.

The emotionally healthy father knows that all fathers have some sexual feelings for their daughters. He does not seduce his little girl, but he does treat her with affection. He kisses her on the cheek, not on her sensualized mouth. He treats her gently to get the message across that he belongs to her mother and that she should learn from her mother how to be a good woman. The reward for learning how to do this is that she will have her own man someday.

Frequently a father can handle his daughter's seductive behavior during her childhood and cope with her announcements that she wants to be his wife, but he has difficulty when she exhibits the same form of behavior during her adolescence. At the time when there is a resurgence of psychological phases in adolescence, a father may find that he is completely incapable of coping with these seductive mannerisms. He may, as a result, berate her for looking sexy and accuse her of being promiscuous. If this attitude of disgust is thrust upon the adolescent girl who is struggling with her sense of autonomy, she may give in and become homosexual at this period of her life.

If the child has had a successful mothering experience and enters eagerly into a mutual love relationship with her father, she is well on the way to becoming a fully mature adult. If her father can see her as a person rather than as his possession, she has a healthy life ahead of her.

Many fathers, however, can not bear to let go of their daughters. Melissa's father was such a man. He delighted in his daughter's adoration of him. He often brought Melissa a gift when he came home from a business trip but forgot to bring some token of love for his wife. That pleased Melissa very much, and she flaunted her gifts in front of the mother. She felt and acted victorious.

To win in life, that is, to be a fully mature genital female, the little girl *must* lose the Oedipal battle over her father. If she wins the favored position with her father, there is no frustration to motivate her into a relationship with her own man. Frustration equals movement toward maturity. Overindulgence of emotional needs leads to stagnated growth.

Melissa's mother often tried to discuss with her husband the extreme relationship between him and their daughter, but he would not take part in it. He simply dismissed her concern, telling her she was just jealous.

Melissa was her father's chief interest and delight. They took long walks after dinner every night, deliberately excluding the mother. Melissa told me that she could not remember if she felt more joy at being alone with her father or because her mother was not invited on these evening strolls. Over the years her contempt for her mother grew.

If her parents were sitting together on the living room couch, Melissa always managed to squeeze in between them and interrupt whatever it was that they were doing or saying. Her father never once said. "I'm talking with your mother now, and you will have to wait." Instead his eyes would light up and he would proclaim, "Here's my little girl."

As a young adolescent, Melissa was a very pretty girl, and she blossomed into a beautiful young woman. Her father was delighted with her growing loveliness and took every opportunity to tell her so. He began taking her out for special Friday night dinners at an elegant restaurant. Her mother was not asked to join them and was actually encouraged to do something else with her evening.

Reality finally intervened when young men began wanting to date Melissa. Against his better judgment, her father let her go out with boys, but only after thoroughly examining each one. He always waited up for her with milk and cookies and asked for a complete accounting of the evening. Very subtly he managed to talk her out of any growing feelings she might have for any of the boys. He listed their faults and made fun of their normal awkwardness. He would mimic their words, actions, and gestures to show her how incompetent these young men were. His message was plain, "I'm the better man, so stay with me."

With this pattern of behavior he was able to control his daughter's love life throughout high school, but he lost the reins when she entered college. He insisted that she call him every other night so he could be sure his "little jewel" was safe. When occasionally Melissa forgot to call, he became distraught and angrily telephoned her dormitory.

As could have been expected, Melissa met and fell in love with a young man her own age. Because she was away from home, the regressive pull of her father lessened enough for her to feel attracted to someone other than her father. After dating for a time, she and the young man decided to marry. Melissa's family was unaware of her strong attachment and her plans, for she had deliberately refrained from telling them.

When Melissa finally announced the happy news to her family, her father turned ashen, clutched at his chest, and suffered a heart attack.

Melissa's father could not fathom the idea of his daughter loving anyone but himself. His heart attack was real, but it was also symbolic. He felt that his heart had been betrayed. Unconsciously he was saying that he would die without her devotion. While he was recuperating, Melissa came to see me. She was filled with guilt over her father's illness and worried that he might die.

Although her father was opposed to her seeking help, we worked together for many months. She was finally able to see how unhealthy her relationship with her father had been. She experienced a great deal of anger at him for wanting two "wives" and for attempting to hold her forever as a dependent child. I explained to her that she had nothing to feel guilty about, because children do not have control over their normal instinctual drives. It is the parents' responsibility to set a healthy course of development.

Melissa and her fiancé married, even though her father tried to use his illness to interfere in their plans. He never really recovered from losing "his darling Missy" into womanhood, and he refused to seek counseling in order to understand his despair.

Parents cannot "lose" their children, for they never actually own them in the first place. They are gifts of nature to be nourished with love and care in order for them to leave home and establish their own, unique, independent lives. This, unfortunately, is a hard reality for many parents to accept.

These case histories illustrate but a small fraction of the symptoms that can occur if parents bungle the job of child rearing. The human animal is subject to so many symptoms of neurosis that it is impossible to describe them all. But human beings are also very resilient. A child to whom considerable damage has been done may yet become a person who can still turn it all around and continue growing from the point where healthy parental direction left off.

In the next chapter, I will discuss some methods by which you can help yourself continue growth that may have been sidetracked. If you find that you cannot accomplish it by yourself, there is therapy to help you. Therapy is no longer only a process for desperate people; it is for any individual who may simply need intelligent and considerate understanding.

V.

SELF-
ANALYSIS

In describing the various personality hang-ups in the psychosexual development of the female, the case histories have not been exaggerated. They are factual accounts of problem situations. Neither are they examples of unusually neurotic people. There is such a wide variety of symptoms of arrested emotional development and so many people in our society are afflicted with some form of neurosis that few can be said to be unusually neurotic.

If you feel that you have problems with living and loving, you can help yourself to overcome them. In order to do so, however, you have to be aware of your own unique symptomatology. There is no need for defensiveness with yourself. In working out your personal program of self-analysis, then, you will have to be coldly honest with yourself. You cannot solve a problem if you refuse to admit its existence.

The program for self-analysis that I shall set out can help you reach full genital maturity. If, however, the task proves too difficult for you to accomplish alone, then I suggest you seek professional help. Fortunately, psychotherapy and counseling no longer have the stigmas attached to them that once inhibited people from seeking help.

Incidentally, many people who seek treatment believe that anyone in the business of psychoanalysis or anyone who does counseling is necessarily expert at his or her job. That is no more true than the belief that because a person has a teaching degree, he is automatically a good teacher. When seeking counseling help, you have a right—indeed you owe it to yourself—to question the therapist about his or her "patient goals." You are not a helpless child, nor need you be a victim of immediate circumstances. You can and should inquire whether the therapist's goal is to help patients become genital personalities or simply to "adjust to society." You should know what the therapist considers to be the most important aspects of life.

There is no such thing as a completely psychoanalyzed person because each person should continue to grow throughout his life. However, it is valid to inquire of a therapist if he or she has had a personal analysis. How did it change his or her life?

In addition, it is important that you feel comfortable with the therapist and not as if you are in an inferior position. Remember that you are spending *your* money and *your* time. You will want to have a close, trusting relationship with your therapist. You should have the feeling that the two of you are partners working together on your problems and that you both have the same goal in mind.

One excellent method of finding a good therapist is to

consult friends who have been in treatment. Has their neurotic behavior changed into healthy patterns of living as a result of their therapy? Have they learned how to handle their own repetition of past history? Have they learned how to love? Have they been able to overcome sexual problems? All of these questions are of vital importance when you are dealing with your emotional life.

Some people prefer a female therapist rather than a male one because they feel it is easier to talk to a woman. The choice is yours, but you must be able to be at ease with whomever you choose. One of my patients recently moved to another city, but since I did not personally know a therapist there to refer her to, I could only suggest that she "shop around." She wrote to me a few weeks later that the first three therapists she visited all "hid" behind their desks and looked "stuffy." The fourth, a man, was busy tacking up his children's drawings on the wall of his office when she entered, and she immediately felt "at home." He turned out to be perfect for her because of his warmth and easygoing nature, qualities she needed in a therapist. He might not have been suitable for someone else with different problems, but he was exactly the right therapist for her.

To begin to help yourself, you will have to sort out in your mind your problems and their ramifications. One requirement for getting things in order is peace and quiet. It is almost impossible to think clearly about such things when other people are around, the television set, the radio, or the record player is on.

So set aside a time for yourself in which you can make a clear, honest appraisal of your life. If you live alone, take a weekend off to get acquainted with yourself. Forget the telephone, let the chores go, and begin your self-assessment program. If you have a family to care for, it is a little more difficult, but again you can arrange to have at least a few hours to yourself. Get a baby-sitter if necessary and go and hide out in a quiet spot such as in a library. You will need privacy in order to recall your personal life history. When doing this, remember that there is absolutely no sense in lying to yourself, as to do so would only defeat your purpose.

Many people carry in their conscious mind comfortable myths about their past. For example, one can go like this: "I had a wonderful family. My parents said I was such a happy child, always laughing. In fact, my nickname was Sunshine! My folks really loved me and each other." Yet the woman who makes that statement can actually be an unhappy person who is denying the facts of her childhood. Such denial is a defense, against facing a truth that is frightening. But if you face the truth of your past and learn how to deal with it in the present, it loses its power to be frightening.

Another very important point is that when you are making the effort to remember your psychological history, it is of no consequence whether the events you recall are accurate in their details. The significance lies in how you perceived events as a child. For instance, Tina's mother always said, "I loved each of my children exactly the same." But Tina *felt* that her mother favored her brothers. What Tina felt is the important emotional fact, not what her mother believed.

Everything that has happened to you from birth is stored away in the unconscious part of your mind. You will never recall all of it but if you engage in the following program, you will be amazed at how much you can remember.

The first step is to make a psychogram of your life. Write down your parents' names, your name and age, and the names and ages of any brothers and sisters you have. The point to recognize is where you fit into the family picture. For example, Anne began with:

> Mother and Father
> Joyce, the oldest—age 21
> Anne, middle—age 19½
> Fred, the baby—age 18½

Just writing this brief sketch made Anne suddenly become aware that she felt squeezed in the family structure. She also remarked that it seemed silly to be still calling her brother, Fred, "the baby" when he was eighteen and a half years old. That idea brought to her consciousness the memory of hating Fred, a memory she had denied all of her life. She hated him because he was always referred to as "the baby"—a term which connotes special needs and attention—and particularly because her mother often referred to Fred as "my baby."

Anne also felt shortchanged because for a time her sister Joyce had had mother all to herself. When Anne was born she had to share her mother with Joyce. And before Anne was out of diapers, along came "the baby." Consequently, Anne felt that she never really had had the special position of the baby in the family. (Of course, Joyce had been jealous when Anne was born, as no child in the state of id-ness likes to share her mother, but when Fred was born, Joyce already was two and a half and did not mind him as much. As a result, she was always closer to Fred than to Anne.)

Remember that the unconscious part of the psyche encourages the conscious part to repeat the early family history. Thus, by working out and studying her psychogram, Anne, who unconsciously had felt squeezed in the middle and frustrated, discovered that as an adult she was getting into similar situations. While she was developing a friendship, the repetiton compulson always urged her to invite a third person into the relationship. More than that, the other person was invariably one who immediately liked the first friend better than Anne. Consequently, Anne would withdraw from the relationship, feeling unwanted by both. What Anne was unconsciously doing was "setting up" each such situation so that she continually repeated her feelings of being left out of her family.

Of course, not all middle children who felt overlooked and frustrated respond to the repetition compulsion in exactly the same way Anne did. Anne's pattern, however, is a very common one, and the differing patterns among people are merely variations on the same theme.

At first Anne felt embarrassed to see that she was constantly playng out her childish feelings. But embarrassment is not important when you are attempting to "see" yourself in a new light. It is the knowledge you acquire about yourself that is important, because it is knowledge that opens the door to real growth. Indeed you probably will feel a sense of excitement as you prepare your psychogram.

After you have diagramed your family structure and your place in it, the next step is to record significant events or traumas that occurred in your family. These events may seem inconsequential to others and even to you after a lapse of years. But whatever comes into your mind should be examined.

Beth's psychogram looked mild to her until she began to add her memories of the past. It soon became clear that she was wasting her adult life in an endless repetition of the past.

Her psychogram looked like this:

Mother	Father
	Beth—age 30	
Mother remarried when I was 18 (but I had already left home)	Father died when I was 16

Beth was a very lonely person. She felt that she could never trust anyone, men or women. The men she chose to have romantic attachments to were always leaving her just when she began to feel love for them.

What had happened to make Beth so lonely? As the only child in the home, she had expected and received an overdose of parental attention. As a result Beth had always felt safe and secure with her parents, and her father's death was an emotional blow from which she had never really recovered.

At the time of her father's death she was an adolescent going through the final resolution of her psychosexual development, which would have culminated in giving up her Oedipal feelings for her father. But when he died at this crucial point in her life, she felt abandoned. At the same time, Beth now came to realize, she had also felt angry with her mother, because her still immature mind told her that if somehow her mother had been stronger, her mother could have kept her father alive. Thus Beth's unconscious message to herself was "See, when you start really loving a man, he goes and leaves you, and since I'm a woman and therefore weak, there's nothing I can do to prevent it. Better to never really let yourself get involved."

In acting on this message, she unconsciously picked out men who she sensed would behave in a way that would prove her point and allow her to repeat over and over again the feeling of abandonment she had suffered from when her father died. To insure that the men in her life would take the step she unconsciously wished for, she became moody, jealous, and excessively demanding at a crucial point in each relationship. Emotionally Beth had stopped growing at the age of sixteen. She kept replaying her father's death and the "failure" of her mother that had resulted in her being left "alone."

It may seem incredible that a person unconsciously sets up situations so many times in a lifetime just to satisfy the unconscious need to repeat one's family history. Remember, that if the original family situation was one of normalcy and happiness, the unconscious seeks to repeat that particular history. No one can complain about that kind of unconscious striving.

When you write down and examine the significant events in your own life, try to recall the feelings you experienced at that time. Sometimes you will be surprised to find yourself overcome by emotion. That is fine. You are only ventilating old feelings that obviously were not allowed to come forth in the original situation.

When Beth finally understood how significant her

father's death was for her, she sobbed for hours. She realized that she had been overcome with anger at her father (for leaving her) and at her mother (for allowing the death to occur). As a result she had never given herself the opportunity to mourn her father's death. By allowing herself to cry and really feel the sense of loss, she freed up the psychic energy she had been misusing for fourteen years. She had been using her emotional energy to repeat the abandonment rather than to fulfill her own life. After her tears, she recounted her deep feelings of love for her father. She was also able to discuss her fear of loss and her anger, and she saw that she had transferred her fear and anger to all men so that she was repeatedly being "abandoned."

Because Beth developed insight into her repetition pattern, she was able to help herself. She could mourn her father and finally give him up. As a result, she was able to continue her growth. She no longer had to choose men that would fit into her neurotic pattern.

In your own psychogram list the members of your immediate family and the personality traits of your parents. Then list the men that have attracted you and describe their habits and personality traits. Perhaps you will discover that you, like Beth, have been making what psychoanalysts call "neurotic choices." If her mother has been the dominating figure in the family, a woman will choose out men with qualities and personality traits similar to those of her mother.

Janice's family psychogram looked like this:

Mother	Children	Father
Nagger	Janice—40	Hardly home
Never satisfied	Bill—37	Traveled a lot
Demanded too much	John—35	Quiet man
Yelled a lot	Wayne—30	Drank too much

Janice's mother was an unhappy woman who felt that the entire burden of raising the family rested on her because of the father's disinterest and frequent absences. Actually she was so loud and vituperative that her husband preferred to be out on the road away from the constant din of the family. When he was at home, he drank to escape his wife's frequent tongue lashings. Janice had felt that the only way she could get any attention from her mother was to be her helper. Therefore she assumed a great deal of the job of caring for her three younger brothers, and even now her brothers still came to her whenever they had even minor problems.

Janice always ended up with men who were demanding and angry people, so it seemed that nothing she did could or would please them enough. Her only resource was to provide them with a kind of mothering as she had always done with her brothers. She admitted that she felt like a "doormat."

When she saw what she was doing—choosing men who had the same personality traits as her mother, she was horrified at herself. Soon she realized that all these years she had unconsciously sought relationships in which she would be victimized by angry men.

Basically Janice herself was a very angry person. Since her early childhood, however, she had felt that she could never show her mother any angry feelings. She had to be a "good" girl and let others take advantage of her. When her anger came out (she wrote it all down), she was also able to have some fantasies that released a great deal of rage she had not even know was buried inside of herself.

Fantasies are an excellent instrument through which to rid oneself of destructive childhood feelings. All children have angry fantasies, such as the thought of bashing their brother or sister with a rock, and many children equate the fantasy with the event. That is, because they *thought* of doing a deed, they believe they have actually done it. As an adult, you may still have vestiges of that kind of reasoning. If so, you will have to recognize the fact that fantasies are only pictures and thoughts in the mind that can do no harm to anyone. More than that, it is normal to fantasize, and indeed fantasies are a very healthy means of expressing aggression.

Angry or murderous fantasies release pent-up and forgotten anger from your childhood, just as the valve on a pressure cooker allows the necessary release of steam. Most people find it difficult to accept the idea that they have aggression. If you will remember our discussion of the id, however, you can no longer deny the fact of your own aggression.

Janice's fantasies had to do with revenge against her mother for being so unloving toward her. She envisioned her mother chained to a wall and unable to talk, still furious at the world but completely helpless. Janice saw that this fantasy revealed that she herself felt helpless as a child, and that she felt like the prisoner of her mother's wrath. In fantasy she did to her mother what she herself had experienced as a child.

Janice had over a hundred fantasies that dealt with her anger toward her mother or were related to the father who had not protected or helped when she was a child. Every time she was able to release her aggression through fantasy she felt herself becoming a stronger person. Through this method she was eventually able to give up being everyone's victim.

The prize for understanding the working of your neurotic pattern is that you can get rid of it and become a loving person. And becoming a loving person leads naturally to the next step—being a loved person.

When you have completed your personal psychogram and relate your life experience to it, you should discover your unique repetition compulsion. By allowing yourself to fantasize, you can work off anger you may feel toward yourself and toward others who have caused you unhappiness. If, however, you persist in feeling guilty about the murderous and revengeful pictures that you may conjure up in your mind, it means that you are resisting progress. The guilty feeling comes from your superego, the emotional structure that represents the parental No's. If your parents did not allow you to express any negative feelings toward them, you will be angry at yourself for having "bad thoughts."

Dorothy's mother was always saying to her, "Don't you dare look at me that way!" or, "If you talk back to me, I'll wash out your mouth with soap!" As a result, Dorothy always tried to hide all of her angry feelings. She went through life smiling at everyone and never talked about anything unpleasant or controversial. But the unexpressed anger of her childhood, as well as the natural anger that comes from the everyday aggravations, had to have some outlet. Since Dorothy was unable to express her anger, it was turned back onto herself. She suffered from headaches, backaches, and other ills, and she always seemed to be cutting herself.

When she tried to release her anger in fantasy, she felt like a traitor. When I was able to convince her that her mother need never know about her fantasies, that everyone had fantasies, and that they were harmless, she was able to relax. Since she had repressed her natural aggression for twenty years, she had a lot of catching up to do. She found it helpful to write down her fantasies, and she soon had filled three notebooks with them. She called these books her "gore books."

Insight into the fantasy is as important as the fantasy itself. The act of fantasy releases aggression, but it is insight into it that advances growth. In our daydream fantasy life there is usually a clue as to how we felt as a child. For example, in the beginning Dorothy's fantasies revolved around her gagged mother having to sit and listen to a tirade by Dorothy. The fantasies made her feel better, but more important, she saw that she still felt like a gagged child and was able to ungag herself. The simple act of telling a waitress that she had served Dorothy the wrong selection made her feel like an adult for the first time in her life. In the past she would have simply accepted the wrong order, smiled at the waitress, and maintained her image of the "good" girl who kept her mouth shut.

Many women mistakenly believe that if they allow any normal aggression to surface, they will necessarily become strident and shrill. But it is emotion that has been repressed that takes on more power than it normally has.

Even though Dorothy was an adult, she was afraid that if she expressed any anger, such as pointing out the waitress's error, she would lose all control, that she would scream, yell, and throw the food at the waitress. That, of course, would be very unsocial behavior and intolerable in the functioning of society. We cannot literally "act out" all of our id impulses, but we can fantasize them.

Dorothy did fantasize attacking the waitress in a rage, but she recognized the nature of the anger in her fantasy. She was angry at the waitress for "not caring for her needs." In reality the waitress represented her mother to her, and it was that old repressed anger at her mother that she felt so strongly. It was her mother she had hated and felt neglected by, not the overworked waitress. (Incidentally, any person who serves food to strangers becomes an unconscious mother figure to the diners. The next time you see someone overreacting to a waitress, you will be able to discern some of his or her mother-child relationship.) Instead of acting out her id fantasy of attacking the waitress (mother), and instead of repressing all her anger at being served the wrong food, Dorothy was able to tell the waitress that she had made a mistake and ask that she be brought the selection she had ordered.

When Dorothy could accept her aggression as a part of her "self," she no longer feared it. She no longer felt that she had to repress normal anger.

Dorothy also allowed herself to fantasize the destruction of anyone who ever made her play the role of the passive, compliant child, and she came to realize that people only treated her that way because she allowed them to do so. Now she noticed that people respected her a great deal more when she presented an honest picture of herself rather than showing a self-effacing mockery of sweetness. And by allowing herself an outlet for aggression, she could begin to grow into a truly loving person. Most of her psychic energy had been used in the repression of her anger so she could present a smiling facade to the world, and that had left little energy for personal growth.

If you have followed the program of self-analysis up to this point, you should have a great deal of information about yourself. You will have a psychogram containing all the important information about your family and your relationship within that human structure. You should have your repetition compulsion clearly defined. You will have a "library" of fantasies expressing your aggression and desires in life.

If you have been open and honest with yourself, your problem should be very obvious to you. Now what?

You must look upon that part of your unconscious that pushes your conscious self to repeat neurotic and unhappy behavior as your internal psychological enemy. It does more damage to your life than any other person can inflict. If you have discovered your personal repetition pattern, you have at the same time acquired knowledge of your unconscious. And if you allow yourself to know your self-destructive unconscious, you can recognize it as a kind of inner voice.

Jeanne was a shy, lonely young woman. She could never bring herself to make a first gesture of friendliness toward anyone, because she felt terrified she would be rejected. Her mother and father had had little time for Jeanne when she was a child, as they spent their lives drinking, yelling, and fighting with each other. Having been surrounded by this chaos all during her childhood, she was always tearful and frightened of the world. Anytime she approached her parents for anything, from food to school supplies or clothes, they told her to "get lost." As a consequence, she was really lost. Even though she managed to grow up physically and even to educate herself, at twenty-eight she was just as lonely and frightened of the world as when she was five years old. And even though now she was able to provide for herself, in a sense she was just as helpless as when she had been left alone in her room, unfed, unclean, and unloved.

Jeanne and I were working on her need to repeat her family's rejection of her when she reported the following incident to me. She was at her office's annual Christmas party and everyone was having a festive time. She saw a pleasant-looking man standing at the bar and thought to herself, "I'll just go over and say hello." But Jeanne said an internal voice told her, "You can't do that. He'll tell you to get lost. Why should anyone want to talk to you." Jeanne knew that this was her unconscious family voice promising her the usual rejection if she made any attempt to break out of her shyness. Her unconscious demand and promise was—"Don't talk to him. Stay inside yourself and then you will be safe!"

Because we had been working on her unconscious pattern, Jeanne had developed some strength with which to fight back against this internal voice. "I'm not afraid anymore!" she said to herself—to her unconscious, really. "I'm going to take a chance and talk to him."

"You'll be sorry!" her inner voice answered. "No one wants you."

Because Jeanne had always followed the demands of her unconscious and remained lonely, she decided that now was a good time to change the habit. Reasoning that she had nothing to lose but her loneliness, she decided to gather her strength and do the opposite of her unconscious directives.

At this party, therefore, she ventured forth to where the man she was attracted to was standing and, to her surprise, he said hello first. Most men are rather shy about talking first to women and usually look for a sign of acceptance—a friendly smile or something more direct like a "Hello" or "Hi"— before they make any advance. But the man Jeanne wanted to meet was very outgoing and gregarious. He was simply interested in people.

Since this is a true story and not a fairy tale, I have to report that this encounter did not start bands playing or lead to the altar for Jeanne. She and the man had a pleasant conversation and there it ended. But Jeanne felt personally victorious. She had gone against her internal voice and she felt stronger and happy. Just one incident did not, of course, destroy the power of her unconscious. After all, it had commanded her life for twenty-eight years, but this was a good beginning.

Because it was formed in childhood, the unconscious never really changes. What can be changed is its effect on your life. You can deprive it of its power and use that energy consciously to enjoy and love life. If, however, you allow your unconscious to live your life for you, then you remain merely a puppet.

If you cannot hear your unconscious directives as clearly as Jeanne did, you can learn to listen through concentration. Again, privacy is necessary. Cut down the noise, lower or turn off the lights, and lie down on the couch. Think about the repetitious patterns in your life. Think of what fears possess you. Allow yourself to indulge in free association. Free association is the best way of voluntarily bringing forth repressed memories. Do not inhibit your mental processes. Even when seemingly insignificant memories or irrelevant words start breaking through, let them come into your conscious mind. They are significant clues. If you feel suddenly drowsy, that is a sign that your unconscious is trying to distract you. Wake up! Try again and again if necessary.

If, when you are lying down and concentrating on hearing your inner voice, nothing happens, then aloud or internally demand an answer of it. Say something like this, "Why are you afraid of depending on anyone?" Listen to the next words that occur to you, as these will be your unconscious answering you. One patient who asked her unconscious that question heard the answer, "You always have to be in control. If you let go and become dependent, you'll fall apart and be abandoned just like when you were a child." She soon saw that by never letting go and allowing herself to love someone she ended up being as alone as she had felt when she was a child, thus satisfying her unconscious.

Such threats from the unconscious that are based on childhood fears and experiences are quite ridiculous. If you believe and respond to them, you will always lose. But if you take the chance and oppose your personal past, you will ultimately win the battle.

We are essentially visual creatures who think and fantasize in pictures from infancy through the rest of our lives. Therefore, dealing with the unconscious is easier if you can personify it, visualizing your internal family manipulator.

Verna had been in psychoanalysis for some time. She had broken out of her neurotic choice pattern, and life was giving her great satisfaction. She had divorced her first husband, who had appealed to her unconscious repetition pattern as a combination of her depriving mother and depressed father. She had gained a sense of independence and eventually married a gentle, loving, happy man. We were in the process of terminating her treatment when she left for a two-week annual honeymoon with her husband.

On her return, she literally burst into the office filled with excitement. She told me the following experience, which has changed the technique of my psychoanalytic work. It has been a remarkable assistance in helping patients to gain emotional strength.

The evening before Verna and her husband were to leave on their romantic vacation, she suddenly came down with all the symptoms of a terrible cold. She had a sore throat, burning eyes, runny nose, and ached all over. Since she had very few illnesses, Verna thought that it might be her unconscious trying to undo her excitement over the vacation. She excused herself from her husband, lay down, and thought, "I'm going to overcome this cold!"

She began her "treatment" by berating her unconscious. To the negative voice of the past she said, "You are *not* going to give me a cold. I work hard all year and this is my vacation. You are not going to interfere with me."

To which her unconscious replied or rather shrieked,

"You wretch! I'm not going to let you have *any* fun. Your nose will be stuffy and your throat will hurt so that you can't enjoy the food and wine. Furthermore, you won't be able to make love!"

Verna was a strong believer in yelling back at her unconscious and she retaliated with: "No, you don't! I'm going to be well!"

Just as that moment she saw with her mind's eye a picture of herself yelling at her unconscious past and she visualized a little gray witch stamping her feet and shrieking at her. Verna said that it made it so much easier to carry on this psychological argument when she could actually "see" her internal enemy.

They yelled back and forth until finally her witch asked, "Then, how about just a sore throat?"

"No, nothing! You get nothing. I'm going to have a good time. You can have this cold, not me!"

This encounter took about half an hour. At the end of that time, all of Verna's cold symptoms had disappeared and she felt strong and healthy.

On her two-week vacation, Verna said, she could call up this image of her unconscious at will and verbally beat it up. She had no unpleasant times during her vacation and really felt on top of the world—and on top of her unconscious. She said that every morning while brushing her teeth, she called the witch into her vision and said, "You aren't going to have any fun with me today. Go scrub a floor, you bitch!" And, in her mind's picture, she would see the witch scurrying away.

This process worked for her and she wanted to share the experience with me. Like a fantasy, her vision of her unconscious had to come out of her repressed childhood memories. I suggested to her that for further understanding we should analyze the image she used to depict her unconscious.

Her free association went like this:—"Little gray witch; it's only three inches tall because I've already analyzed away a lot of its aggression, otherwise it would be human size. The witch looks like the witch from Snow White—the one who wanted to kill Snow White because she was lovely. You know, the witch always looked in the mirror—oh, my mother was always looking in the mirror—it's her!—she tried to kill my sexuality—my love of life—that's who my gray witch is!"

From then on I asked my patients to "see" (without thinking about it first) what came into their visual scene when they thought about what their own unconscious enemy would look like. It was quite a revelation because I found that each person was able to see something and begin to relate to that image. Each individual's unique psychological history gave him a unique picture.

One young man saw a blue fog surrounding him. In his free association he discovered that his mother, who nearly always dressed in blue and was extremely possessive, was the core of his unconscious. This suffocating fog symbolized his enemy.

A young student with Lesbian problems could not complete a term paper, so she put down all of her voices and tried to visualize her unconscious force. She saw an enormous Viking woman who pointed a spear at her and said, "You cannot succeed!" The young woman thought, "If you are so big and frightful, I must have seen you that way as a child. But I'm not a child anymore. You are just a visualization of my unconscious.

So, I can shrink you and put you aside and finish this damn paper!" Which she promptly did.

Some patients have seen their unconscious represented as animals, including bears, cats, and weasels; the choice depended upon their emotional history. What you visualize is not as important as the fact that a visualization makes it easier to fight it out with those unconscious forces that plague your life.

The methods I have described have helped many patients to overcome their childhood problems and free themselves to live without repeating the traumas of the past. If you are willing to put forth the energy and time that it takes, you can do it too. As Jeanne, the shy, rejected girl had learned, you have nothing to lose but your own unhappiness.

VI.

ORGASM

Orgasms are nature's gift to the female to enable her to fully enjoy her sexuality. There is no physiological reason for a woman to have an orgasm. The male must have an orgasm in order to produce semen to fertilize the female egg, but the female, being the recipient of the semen, has only to accept the fluid into her body in order for the process of creation to begin. However, unlike most other animals, we humans do not have intercourse just to reproduce. As complicated structures, we have many reasons for intercourse, ranging from relieving anxieties to sharing love feelings.

You can see from our study of human psychosexual development that we are sensualized beings from the very beginning of life. The first zone of excitement and pleasure is the mouth. After completing one's development, the center and core of the sensual feelings rests mainly in the genitals. If you have matured into a full woman, you should be able to enjoy a feeling of sexuality all the time. It is feeling a sense of oneself as a female that allows you to enjoy your body and all of the pleasures it provides. Sensuality includes the experience of pleasure in combing your hair, showering, feeling your skin, and the way you move. It is feeling your body's presence in relationship to others. It is feeling joy at being touched by a man, whether it be a loving caress on your face or the joining together of penis and vagina in making love. It is being aware of your sense of excitment about all of life's experiences. It is being able to love the concept of men in general and in creating a relationship with one in particular. It is accepting one's body as a beautiful and unique object. It is building your soul and letting it be in harmony with nature by experiencing orgasms when having sexual intercourse.

Orgasms are a natural outcome of sexual excitement, a release of emotional energy, and the culmination of sexual arousal. It is therefore healthy to experience orgasms and unpleasant not to let nature take its course. A woman who cannot experience orgasm is frigid.

The term "frigid woman" has been thrown about carelessly for years. It has been used to insult a suffering woman or to disparage a woman who may have aspirations in life that seem to threaten men. In addition to being an unpleasant phrase, it is inaccurate because it implies that the woman referred to is cold and heartless.

I have known many women who deeply desired to have an orgasm but whose emotional hang-ups prevented them from achieving it. Some have been very sweet women, who loved their husband and children and were possessed of kind and giving natures. Too much emphasis has been placed on the problem of frigidity, making many females think they are hopelessly neurotic if they cannot have an orgasm.

Some people mistakenly think that frigid means the inability to have intercourse, but there are many women who can accept penetration but do not experience any emotional feelings during intercourse. Other women really love their men and enjoy the marvelous sense of closeness between them during lovemaking, and yet they never reach a climax. That does not necessarily make them neurotic, nor should they feel like failures in life.

Some females experience pain during intercourse that cannot be attributed to a physical cause. The pain is a symptom of some mechanism at work in the woman's unconscious that wants to make sex painful and unpleasant for her. She may be a loving person on all other levels, and to label her "frigid" forever is unreasonable and cruel.

The intent of this chapter is to explain the capabilities of sexual pleasure that females are born with, not to put down anyone with sexual problems. If you cannot experience an orgasm, stop thinking "I am frigid. I'll always be frigid, hence I'm no good!" That is basing a person's worth solely on her sexual performance and therefore is an invalid judgment. Think of your inability to have an orgasm as a symptom of something deep within your unconscious that forces you to withhold from yourself a natural pleasure. As you know from previous chapters, you can learn to recognize your own unconscious motivations. It is possible to break out of the habit of not experiencing orgasms.

If you have your psychogram and repetition compulsion mapped out, you will be able to see how hang-ups occurred during your childhood. Soon you will also be able to see how they affect your ability to enjoy sex or achieve orgasm. In the unconscious mechanism to repeat the family history is also the desire to continue family attitudes. Verna's mother was a woman who distrusted men. She never allowed herself to get emotionally close to a man or to experience sexual pleasure, even though she married three times. She sought men who would take care of her financially and accept her as she was. She put on an act of being loving toward them, but that was all it was—an act.

Verna's mother always said, "Men are just interested in one thing." When Verna asked her mother what that "thing" was, all she received for an answer was a sly smile and the words "You'll find out soon enough." Verna couldn't wait. As a young adolescent, she hoped that the "thing" her mother so much despised was romance and its sexual expression, because that was all she was really interested in. As a matter of fact, she was consumed with sexual fantasies.

Through her psychogram she realized she had escaped from completely identifying with her mother only because of an aunt who had had a great influence on her life from the time she was born. Her aunt enjoyed and deeply loved her husband. While Verna's mother was busy manipulating men for financial security and "paying" them by allowing them to have their "disgusting way," Aunt Louise was enjoying a loving life. Even her physical characteristics were in contrast to those of Verna's mother. She seemed to glow with good health and happiness and her features had a softness that contrasted with the tight features of Verna's mother, who was always busy dominating all situations. However, in her unconscious mind Verna held many of her mother's attitudes of which she was not consciously aware.

When Verna was an adolescent, she masturbated regularly while having fantasies of being made love to by a handsome celebrity. She had clitoral orgasms and enjoyed them. Her mother had never given her any admonitions against masturbtion, because she was educated enough to know that it is harmless. She herself masturbated, and, in fact, that was the only way she was able to have an orgasm; on her own, and never while she was with any of the three men she had married. Verna knew this as she had overheard her mother and aunt discussing it one day. Her mother had said, "I'm not going to let any man see me wide open and vulnerable while I'm coming!"

Verna's aunt had replied, "But then you're all alone, just having an orgasm without the pleasure of sharing it with your man."

"Men only want to dump their load, so why should I share my sex with them?" Verna's mother retaliated.

Verna retreated from that scene, puzzled and wondering who was right, her mother or her aunt. Were men like her mother described them or were they like Aunt Louise seemed to see them? It was obvious which of the two women was the happier person. What kind of a man would marry a woman who just wanted to be taken care of financially and had to pretend in order to have sex, rather than actually enjoy it? Not much of one, Verna decided. Indeed Verna's mother's life proved her own unconscious right by choosing men who did only want to "dump their load."

The part of Verna's unconscious that contained her mother's attitudes toward men allowed her to experience orgasm while masturbating because that meant having sex alone.

To digress for a moment—what does a clitoral orgasm resulting from masturbation feel like? There have been many studies that try to chart the female orgasm. What happens to the woman's heartbeat, blood pressure, nipples, etc., etc., have all been graphically described. Since orgasm is a personal physical and emotional experience, however, all these tests and charts are useless to the woman who wants to know just how it feels. It is difficult to describe such feelings, but I will attempt an explanation.

A woman begins by rubbing her clitoris in a circular motion by hand or with an object. Some women's clitorises are supersensitive to direct touch so they can be masturbated through cloth. After a few moments, the time depending upon the person, a feeling of physical excitement and intense pleasure begins to grow in the clitoris and continues growing as long as the motion is continued. When her orgasm begins, a female usually has to continue the stimulation for the orgasm to continue, whereas once a man's orgasm starts it continues automatically until the fluid is released.

The clitoral orgasm feels good and the body experiences a release. It feels satisfied and refreshed. The sensations in the clitoris then diminish. The feeling of physical pleasure after orgasm stays centered around the clitoris for some minutes. Unlike men, women can masturbate and achieve clitoral orgasms as often as they wish.

A woman can also have a clitoral orgasm if a man strokes her genitals. It can also be experienced when she rubs against something pleasurable or even when riding a horse.

Because society has established rules about adolescent expression of sexuality, masturbation is an excellent outlet for young people who are trying to deal with their sexual feelings. For women without men, masturbation relieves sexual frustration. Since it is essentially a lone activity, however, it does not do much for the genital female's need to commune with a man on all levels.

Verna's first sexual encounters after the usual adolescent years of kissing and petting were pleasant but confusing. She was nineteen and living away from home. She fell in love with a man who, because of her repetition compulsion, was like her father and stepfathers. The man was attracted by her beauty and wanted her as an "adornment" in his life. He was a "load dumper," but Verna could not see the similarity between him and her mother's husbands. Actually it was not Verna who had selected this man but rather her unconscious (her mother) who had made the neurotic choice.

After a period of kissing and caressing during her first serious sexual encounter, Verna was very sexually excited. The man took her to bed and as soon as he had entered her vagina and pushed against her clitoris, Verna had a clitoral orgasm which was the best she had ever experienced. It was better than her previous orgasms because a man had done it with his penis and with some lovemaking associated with it, rather than Verna having achieved it by herself. She moaned in pleasure and a moment after she experienced her orgasm, her partner had an ejaculation. He then rolled over and went to sleep. Even with him in bed beside her she felt strangely alone. He was not happy for her or interested in her reaction. He did not want to discuss their mutual enjoyment, all he wanted was to go to sleep. She felt alive and excited about a new sensual experience and she wanted to share her feelings with him.

After several similar encounters with this man, Verna decided to visit her Aunt Louise. She asked her aunt what lovemaking should be like for the man and the woman. Her aunt had known very few women who really enjoyed their sexuality as much as she did, and she could see that now was the time to share her genital female knowledge with her niece. She told Verna that because of the way the body is structured, anyone can have a physical orgasm but that making love has much more significance than just releasing body tensions.

As Verna thought about it she realized that her aunt and uncle shared a tender foreplay whenever they were together. They were always touching each other, sometimes just a pat but often stopping to hug each other while passing in the room. They were aware of each other's need for affection. Because they loved each other, both were always looking for ways to express that love. That does not mean they were crawling all over each other and kissing every time that they looked at one another. Rather they evidenced a gentle, mutual awareness of each other.

Louise said that sometimes she began their lovemaking, at other times her husband initiated it. They had been making love together for some years and had learned where and how the other enjoyed being caressed during their foreplay.

The pleasures of two bodies joined in sexual intercourse were described to Verna. When two people are communicating their love and pleasure with each other by making love, the whole body feels sensualized. Mouths are joined together, the breasts and nipples of the female rub against the man's chest, legs join, and the vagina and the penis rub together and fit in a perfect combining of opposite organs. When erect, the penis tilts forward and fits the scoop-shaped vagina of a woman who is reclining.

Much to Verna's surprise, she was told by her aunt that a man who is concerned with his partner's pleasure as well as his own is not going to have an orgasm as soon as he enters her vagina. He may be intensely excited and feel like coming immediately but he enjoys his body sensations and his woman's orgasms to such an extent that he waits. After a man has his orgasm, the penis loses its erectness and he usually can no longer continue the act of intercourse. After a woman experiences orgasm, however, she can continue to have intercourse and even have more orgasms.

If a woman says there is no difference between a clitoral and a vaginal orgasm, or that there is no such thing as a vaginal orgasm, then she has never had a vaginal experience. And if a man claims that there is no vaginal orgasms, it is simply that he has never been with a woman who had vaginal orgasms. The vaginal orgasm is a fact, and the difference between the two kinds of female orgasms is profound. All orgasms feel good but vaginal orgasms are much better.

It should be noted that there is a physical difference between how the clitoral and vaginal orgasms are reached. To achieve clitoral orgasm, the clitoris is physically stimulated, and little or no emotional involvement is necessary. The vaginal orgasm does depend on emotional involvement. In fact, the simple act of intercourse, without a complete sense of giving and receiving, usually does not produce an orgasm in most women. There is nothing within the vagina itself that triggers vaginal orgasms. The experience is so tied up with the woman's emotional state that it is generated by what we might say is the heart. Indeed, a vaginal orgasm can be experienced without physical contact. Some genital women I know experience vaginal orgasms in dreams, while reading a moving love poem, or while looking at a scene of beauty.

Because it takes so many years to mature, however, it is not unusual for young women to experience only clitoral orgasms until they are in their mid-twenties. If there are no deep unconscious conflicts, the mature female will then go on to experience vaginal sensations and orgasms. So if a woman is having clitoral orgasms she is not sexually deficient. She is having orgasms and is enjoying and sharing as much of herself as she is able to do.

Women who reach vaginal orgasms, however, tend to describe them poetically. Louise was no exception, as she thoroughly enjoyed her sexual feelings and her emotional freedom to have them. As she told Verna: "It's a total, exquisite experience when you are making love with a man whom you love and trust and who loves you. Your whole body feels great excitement and sensual pleasure during intercourse. You can feel his penis inside of you, moving in and out of your vagina and you squeeze it lovingly with your pelvic muscles. Slowly but certainly an excitement begins to mount deep within your body and is felt all along the vagina walls. Then, waves of intense pleasure, pounding waves, flow first through your vagina and the entire genital area. Then they flow into your arms and legs and you push your body as close as possible into the man. You have the desire to seek more of his penis, because it is giving you such ecstatic joy. You want to cry or laugh or yell out loud at the wonderful sensations you feel in your vagina and throughout your body!"

An orgasm such as Louise described can last from fifteen seconds to an hour or more. Whatever its time duration, it is a total body and soul experience that lifts the woman to soaring heights of passion. It is a true sharing of all of the self. Any man who has this kind of joyful life-enriching sexual encounter with his woman is happy to give such pleasure to her, and he will try to give her the opportunity to have as many orgasms as she desires.

It used to be considered the height of sexuality for both parties to achieve orgasm simultaneously. That is a wonderful experience, but since the orgasm is a very personal happening, many people, rather than being consumed by their own feelings and sensations, want to be fully aware of his or her lover having an orgasm so they can enhance their partner's pleasure.

It was after this enlightening conversation with her aunt that Verna came into treatment with me. Her object as she explained it, was to become as much like her Aunt Louise as possible. She had a sucecssful analysis and developed into a fully mature genital woman. Incidentally, she told me that when she experienced her first vaginal orgasm, it felt like she was reborn.

If you have problems having the beautiful sexual experiences that all women are capable of having, you can use the tools of self-analysis to help overcome your difficulties. We all transfer our feelings for our parents to the rest of the world. For example, Verna's mother experienced all men as "users of women" because that was the way she experienced her own father. If your experience with your father was painful and, if in the Oedipal period, the rejection was too severe, then you have probably transferred your childhood feelings to all men.

Essentially the woman's ability to experience orgasms with a man is based on the idea of fusion with him and a willingness to allow herself to be emotionally open— and thus vulnerable. You can see that during a vaginal orgasm a woman gives up emotional control of herself and gives in to complete sexuality. Of course the man is also vulnerable during orgasm, but if your unconscious wants to impede your sexual experience, it either distorts the meaning of that fact or causes you to overlook it. Remember that the unconscious directs you to repeat the past. It promises you that if you maintain control, you will be able to protect yourself and be safe from harm. Engage in free association here and try to determine what actual harm you imagine will occur if you allow yourself full sexual pleasure.

Bernice was a beautiful woman who had modeled for pornographic magazines and had had uncounted sexual encounters from the age of sixteen. She was entranced with the movies and with Hollywood. As confident as Bernice appeared with men, her seductiveness and willingness to go to bed with almost anyone, all masked a basic fear. Bernice was essentially afraid of men and actually hated them. She put on her Hollywood glamour act in bed and pretended to enjoy each man's caresses complete with moans and sighs, body-posturing, and vigorous movement. Her lovers thought that they must be very accomplished to arouse such a beautiful creature.

Bernice related that she was really making fools of these men because they were so easily deceived by her act. In reality she controlled the entire situation. The men who were her partners became the weaker ones when they had their orgasms. Bernice always faked an orgasm, for she was not interested in letting go and thus losing control. They never knew that she gave nothing of herself.

Bernice came for treatment because of what happened to her one evening. While she was going through her usual act, her lover, who was a sensitive man, removed his body from hers and told her that he did not know why she was putting on such a performance but he did not care to be used in that way. She became very alarmed and tried to defend herself to him, but he knew that his evaluation of her was accurate. Since she could not share her feelings with him, he left her. He said he was sorry she had to be alone, as he truly felt she was a special person underneath all that camouflage of sexiness.

Although she felt panic at having been caught in her game, Bernice was also grateful that someone had pointed out that she needed to change. She was intelligent enough to accept what he said rather than resent or ignore it.

What Bernice had been doing was simply a repeat performance of her childhood and adolescent years; she did to men now what her father had done to her when she was a child. She looked on all men as being essentially like her father.

When she was a child, her father always encouraged her to put on shows for him. He wanted to see her dance and sing and strike sexy poses. He encouraged her to be an exhibitionist and even when she became an adolescent he often demanded that she dance for him. In her unconscious mind there was fixed the idea that "men like a show." She felt no guilt or embarrassment at posing nude in front of cameras because unconsciously she felt approval by her father. However, this was all her father did approve of—acting sexy, not engaging in sex.

When Bernice entered her adolescence, her father felt threatened by her sexual growth. As a result, he traumatized her in brutal fashion. Long before she had had any sexual experience, he began to call her a "slut-whore" and accused her of being promiscuous. He berated her daily and beat her when she wore any clothes he considered "revealing." This went on for several years until she finally left home. By this time she felt worthless, terrified of experiencing her sexuality, and, for some unknown reason, full of guilt. She was emotionally confused because of her father's dichotomous attitude, encouraging her to perform for him but at the same time punishing her for being "forward."

The problem, of course, was that her father could not handle his feelings of attraction to his budding young daughter. Instead of dealing with his feelings, which were neither abnormal nor unusual, he turned away in disgust. He made her into a "bad" girl to cover up for his own feelings. So Bernice as an adult repeated this pattern of behavior by fooling men and performing for them just as she had for her father. When she got into contact with her unconscious voice during free association, she realized that she feared if she ever let a man know that she was sexual and had feelings, he would attack her in some brutal way.

It took Bernice some time to work through her feelings of being "bad" and of being terrified of men and their supposed capacity for brutality. However, since she was strongly motivated to grow up and out of her empty life, she was able to change. She admitted that her life was just a merry-go-round of men and games. It had no real meaning and substance. She wanted something more for herself.

Later she contacted the man who had first confronted her with herself and apologized to him for what had happened. They became friends and then true lovers.

Bernice said that even though she had had intercourse with many men, she was an emotional virgin. For her, sex was a combination of theatrical performance in which she repeated her relationship with her father and a way of getting back at him.

Because of her development in treatment, she experienced clitoral orgasms with her lover and was able for the first time to really enjoy sexual sharing. But she always argued with me that vaginal orgasms were a myth.

As Bernice grew in her analysis, she became more and more open with her lover on all levels of their relationship. This involved being honest in discussing her feelings and fears with him. It meant working together for their mutual happiness. It meant openly sharing herself in bed.

One day she came to her appointment with a radiant smile and glowing eyes. "I came! I really did!" she exclaimed. "It's really true about vaginal orgasms!" We did not get much analytic work accomplished that day. We were just two women exchanging views about the joys of being female.

We must all continue to grow in our emotional life until our deaths. There is no age at which one can say, "Now I'm completely grown." If you are a woman in your thirties or forties and have had only clitoral orgasms or if you have not experienced any kind of orgasm, there is no rule that you cannot move forward in your development.

Working on your unconscious will expose the wishes that are keeping you from achieving fulfillment as a woman. Lie down in a quiet place and listen to what comes to your mind about the general topic of men. Do not be alarmed if some of your thoughts and feelings sound strange and childish. For example, one patient related that much to her surprise she discovered that she equated men with her own death. Her free associations went like this: "Men—they want to own you—they own you with their power—penis power—make you a slave— I'll never let one of them inside me so he can own me— being owned is a kind of death of the self."

Her father had been an extremely possessive man who looked upon his daughter as an object he owned. She defined her sexual stirrings toward him during her Oedipal periods as a part of his power to own her. From this she drew the conclusion that all men could control and own her if she let herself feel any sexual pleasure. She was surprised that this came out of her unconscious because she had always consciously liked men. She even had what she considered a happy marriage. She enjoyed lovemaking but had never climaxed. She realized that she was really withholding her "core of self" from her husband because her unconscious threatened that he would enslave her. As a matter of fact, for years her husband had felt that she was holding back her center of self and had felt lonely in their sexual relationship.

Fortunately my patient had married a man who had her mother's characteristics rather than her father's possessiveness. Now seeing the absurdity of the unconscious threat, she was able to laugh at it and finally let go. She was then able to give and to share her sexuality with her husband.

Your own free associations will be as unique as you are. You must free associate in order to expose what is going on in your unconscious. After you have worked through the topic of men in general, let your mind freely associate about particular men in your life, such as your grandfather, father, brother, husband, son, or friend. You may discover yourself using an identifying phrase similar to the one Verna's mother used—"All men are—" What? Selfish, cruel, childish, weak, dangerous? Whatever negative characteristics you attribute to men as a group reflect your feelings about your father or father-substitute transferred to all men.

All men are not the same. Each one is a unique person just as each woman is unique. If you look upon all men as "beasts," then, of course, that is all you will see, rather than giving them a chance as individuals to show and share what they are.

The next question for your free-association thoughts will be: "What will happen to me if I give up my inner controls and allow myself to have orgasms?"

Jane's answer to herself was "You'll fall apart!" She felt that if she allowed herself to depend on a man for pleasure, the feelings of infantile dependency would overwhelm her. She feared that she would fall apart emotionally if she had an orgasm. She unconsciously equated "letting go of feelings" with being a helpless child.

In the free thoughts that come into your mind, try to be objective with yourself and press on. If giving in means to you letting the man have "power," then say to your inner voice, "Yes, and then what?"

To allow your unconscious to convince you that you may not enjoy orgasms is ultimately to be self-punitive. No matter what the unconscious reasoning is, you are its victim. It is you who receives no sensual pleasure. It is you who suffer.

By exposing and exploring the attitudes you internalized as a child, you can gain sufficient insight into your motivations to free yourself from their destructive force. The ability to change is one of the most valuable qualities we human beings are endowed with.

VII.

MARRIED
LIFE

There should be classes beginning in grade school to instruct young people about the meaning of feelings and how important they are in life. Junior high and high school students would benefit greatly from help in understanding their psychological development and the periods of stress they produce. A logical outcome of these instructions would be classes that dealt with being an adult and how to handle the responsibilities that come with growing up.

One of the most meaningful responsibilities an adult accepts is marriage and yet this commitment is rarely discussed with children during their formative years. More emphasis is placed on achieving a place in the business or professional world. It has become the custom to equate a good job with a satisfactory life. Certainly work well done should be a source of heightened self-esteem to the person performing it, but, if his emotional life is unsatisfactory, he is merely an unhappy individual who makes money. It is not material, social, or business success that makes a person feel satisfied in life. Our sense of being happy is directly connected with our loving and being loved.

You can see then how beneficial classes and discussion on feelings and relationships would be to growing youngsters.

As a child, Jason had the continuing fantasy that one day he would be rich and famous and then someone would really love him. This fantasy was encouraged by the attitude of his parents and teachers. For example, he was made to feel that he was a worthless person unless he had all A's on his report card. Later, although he was basically a romantic and poetic young man, he was pushed by parental pressure into becoming a doctor. Both of his parents had their own motives for doing this. Jason's mother wanted to be able to brag about her son being a professional man. She also had her own private fantasy of eventually being supported by him. Jason's father had wanted to become a doctor himself but had failed in school. So Jason accepted his parents' version of his life and did, in fact, become rich and quite famous for his work in medical research.

By the age of forty-five, Jason was the embodiment of the American dream of fame and riches. Yet he was plagued by doubts and loneliness. Jason's story is not an unusual one. Let us take a closer look at him and his life.

Imagine Jason sitting in his comfortable, spacious home. The maid is in the kitchen preparing dinner. The gardener is within view, tending the garden. Jason's wife is at a meeting. Jason himself has been looking at some brochures, trying to decide which car he should buy. But nothing he sees, hears, or is trying to plan satisfies him anymore. He asks himself why he should feel so damned lonely and unfulfilled?

He kept denying to himself that for years he had not really loved his wife. Having repeated his childhood family pattern, Jason had married a highly ambitious woman very much like his mother. Jason's wife loved him for his fame and wealth. She enjoyed the role of the successful doctor's wife. She was happy to be free of material worries and enjoyed belonging to clubs, having a large house in the nicest section of town, and receiving the automatic respect of the community.

Jason's feeling of loneliness had really hit him at one of their frequent catered cocktail evenings, filled with noise and emptiness. A young woman had approached him in the crowd and not knowing that he was a famous doctor simply began to talk to him as an individual. She was very honest and direct in her approach. She told him she had felt attracted to him as soon as she entered the room because she sensed a gentle kindness about him. He did not look as if he belonged there in that group, she said.

As Jason talked to her, impressions and emotions surfaced that, along with his poetry and other attempts to express his feelings, had been buried since his adolescence. Having become used to being accepted for his performance and reputation, he somewhat defensively told her who he was and what he was known for in medical research.

She appeared unimpressed by this recital of his accomplishments and continued to relate to him as a pleasant, gentle man. This was quite upsetting to Jason, his sense of personal worth was all tied up with his achievement of wealth and fame. To have another person dismiss those qualities was very disturbing.

Jason's wife did not notice the interchange between Jason and the young woman. She was too preoccupied with how she looked, with what other women were wearing, with what she was saying and what others were saying. She was not, therefore, aware that when the young woman left the party she told Jason, "My name is Nadine and I feel that this meeting was special between us. You're a good person."

These few words had rocked Jason. They had interjected some new feelings into his neatly packaged life. After all, he told himself, a doctor was not supposed to fall in love, he was supposed to take care of everyone. Jason even had a terrifying vision of the community banishing him forever if he were to be so foolish as to act on his feelings.

What happened was that he did act on his feelings, and he did fall in love—but only after he could accept the fact that the woman loved him for himself, not for what he had done.

His soul began to grow and he developed the creativity his parents had tried to stifle. He began to use his creative gifts in writing and allowed his feelings of romance to come forward and be enjoyed.

I will not detail Jason's struggles against conformity and social taboos, the divorce and settlement arrangements. They all happened but eventually Jason and Nadine were married. Now he is a well-known poet and writer of prose. He no longer has a big house, a new car every year, a maid, a gardener, and giant fees to pay to accountants to take care of his finances. His first wife, incidentally, remarried and is very comfortable in her new role of "the politician's wife." She is still busy going to meetings and parties and it is said that she hopes her new husband will be the next governor of the state.

Jason has become a happy fulfilled man who went against tremendous forces of social and family pressure to seek his own way in life. Now the foundation of his meaningful life is based on his love and relationship with Nadine.

Jason's family considered what he did as selfish, but there are times when we all should be healthily selfish in planning our lives. Jason had been contributing nothing to himself and less to the world than he was capable of. But in his newfound identity and with his new sense of worth, he not only enjoys the benefits of being loved and loving, he gives it back to the world. He is able to share his feelings through his writing.

We are all programmed to "get married and settle down" when we grow up, and it is part of the repetition compulsion to find a mate who has qualities similar to those of our parents.

For women, particularly, getting a man and marrying is what is emphasized in our culture, but not much is said about what to do after this has been accomplished. Of course it is sadly evident what happens afterward to a great many couples—they get a divorce.

Of course not everyone gets married and thankfully the social stigma of the "old maid" is gradually declining. Becoming married does not automatically mean that a woman is a genital person nor does the state of being unwed mean nongenitality. I have known nuns who were genital women. They devoted their maturity and love to the world and its needs rather than lavishing it on a person or a family. I have known genital women who never married because they never felt they had ever found the appropriate mate. Some women do not marry because they are absorbed in their careers. None of these reasons should make them outcasts.

There are many individual reasons why some people never marry. Some reasons are neurotic, of course, but never assume that an unmarried person is "sick."

I once knew a beautiful, warm, and talented woman in her thirties about whom people constantly wondered since she apparently was not married. I happened to know that she had been married but the marriage had been ended by her husband's tragic death. Their relationship had been a deep and loving one, and she had told me that although their time together had been brief, it had given her such total satisfaction that she just did not feel the necessity to seek out marriage again. She was not an unhappy, morose woman living in the past; she had an active career, a few close friends, and a satisfying social life. But she also had the warm memory of her husband and their love and that was sufficient for her.

The point of all this, of course, is to remind you not to be hasty in your judgments of others. There are often very good reasons why people are unmarried. However, it is impossible to deny that marriage is very popular in our culture. When I use the term "marriage" I am including all male-female relationships that are constructed around the commitment of joining together two lives for the purpose of living a meaningful, loving life. So whenever two people establish this sense of togetherness and family, the legalities of marriage licenses, formal ceremonies, and society's blessing are of little concern. I speak of the state of being emotionally married to another person.

As you have seen, because the psychosexual developmental process consumes a lengthy period of time, a person does not grow up and become an independent person until he is beyond adolescence. The final resolution and coming together of personality during adolescence does not make this period conducive to a successful marriage. Two eighteen-year-olds who marry are usually quite different people by the time they reach their mid-twenties. Often they turn out to be strangers to each other.

Because of the great emotional demands placed on two people who enter marriage, it is appropriate that each should be a "together" person. In other words, each should be mature before entering into this adult arrangement in living.

We begin life as dependent beings. If parents do their job in a kind, loving and understanding way, the older adolescent should be able to leave home and become an independent person. That means a person who can take care of himself; who can work and take care of the daily chores that need to be done. He should have the ability to make decisions on his own and handle life's problems. These problems may range from making dental appointments and dealing with an automobile accident to relating to peers and authority figures. He should be able to cope with his feelings in a mature way. Being mature precludes acting like a dependent child and running home to one's parents in every crisis.

None of these ego accomplishments happen all at once. A young person should have some years of living alone and experiencing life as an independent person in order to master situations and grow a sense of personal worth and accomplishment.

He should meet many different men and women and develop different relationships. If a woman accepts her sexuality, she should be able to enjoy sexual experience with the different men she may love. Until recently most girls did not have intercourse unless they were married or at least engaged. Indeed, consciously or unconsciously too many girls got married just to be able to experience sex. Certainly that is a ridiculous and ultimately sad reason for making a lifelong commitment.

Because of their repressed sexual background, many adults were horrified at the advent of modern contraceptives. They assumed that all young people spent eighty percent of their time indulging in sex. This proved not to be the case. Sex had now become simply one part of a relationship. It was no longer a mysterious and forbidden act.

So today young people think more realistically about sex. It is another means of achieving intimacy and closeness necessary to sustaining a love relationship. The young people I see today are mainly concerned with their ability to establish a loving relationship with another person rather than being sidetracked by the issue of "should I or should I not have sexual experiences."

If a young woman has had the opportunity to experience life as an independent person, she should be ready to enter into marriage as an adult rather than as a child seeking someone to substitute for her parents.

Marriage is a bond. It is an exclusive private arrangement between two people. The vows of matrimony involve giving up one's parents and devoting one's life to a new family unit. In a marriage ceremony the father usually "gives away the bride." This is a social custom which in effect publicly resolves the father's Oedipal claims on his daughter.

Marriage is a commitment. Husband and wife promise to love each other, care for each other's needs with thoughtfulness and concern. A marriage symbolizes that here are two people who wish to join together and become even better people because of that joining.

The basic ingredient of marriage should be love for each other and a mutually healthy, mature dependence on each other. Loving someone means that his or her happiness is essential to your happiness. Many people fear the word "dependency" because they do not understand the meaning of the word in terms of a mature relationship. They are afraid they will feel an infantile dependency such as they experienced with their parents. However, if a woman is allowed to become a full genital person and grow a sense of independence from her parents, then she can allow herself to depend on a man for love and joy and can do this without feeling like a child.

When mature men and women love one another, they say, "I am dependent on you for love and affection and my fullest sense of well-being. I am not afraid of these feelings because they are mutual. We are also separate people in that we can have differing opinions and capabilities. But when it comes to feelings of sharing love and life, we are totally together." This credo is what makes marriage a beautiful and growing life adventure. If mutual and mature dependency is absent from a marriage, trouble looms in the future.

Another benefit of waiting to make a marriage commitment until you have matured into an independent genital person is that by then you will have had an opportunity to catch repetitive neurotic patterns or choices in your life. And through self-analysis or professional treatment, you will have also been able to alter those negative characteristics.

The unconscious repetition compulsion is most clearly evidenced in marriage choices. People who do not know their unconscious mechanisms, invariably repeat their family patterns by marrying someone like their mother or father.

For instance, this is what happened with Doris whose father was an alcoholic. You will remember that an alcoholic is a person who is stuck in the oral phase of development. Doris was so anxious to avoid anyone who was like her father that she refused to date anyone who even drank socially. However, she did marry a man who was addicted to food. He was not an alcoholic, but he was similar to her father in that he was an oral personality. He ate all the time and was just as infantile as her father had been.

There is no escape from the repetition compulsion unless you gain awareness of and master your unconscious and its drives.

Let us return to Jason and Nadine and look at how a successful marriage works. Many people assume that after the vows are spoken, a marriage just goes on by itself and requires no effort. In any endeavor of life, work is the necessary ingredient for success. This is especially true of a marriage. Marriage is a daily experience that requires close attention if it is going to make two people happy.

Your best friend should be your marriage partner.

A friend respects your rights as an individual. He or she does not try to control your thoughts and feelings but does try to be aware and sensitive to your moods. A friend tries to empathize and sympathize with you and your problems. A friend cares about your sensitivities and avoids hurting you. Most of all, a friend is on your side and holds the friendship more dear than any differences the two of you may have.

Jason and Nadine, by being open and honest with each other about everything developed a deep and binding friendship along with their love for each other. As with all people, when they began to live together, some irritations became obvious. We all think the way we do things, from brushing our teeth to writing checks, is the right way. Jason and Nadine had their minor differences. Neither of them, however, wanted or needed to control the other. After all, there is no mutual relationship if one or the other partner feels that he or she must be the boss. Being or having a boss over the relationship is a regression to the parent-child relationship. Jason and Nadine talked about what they did not like in each other's habits. Their discussions were not threatening to their marriage because their purpose was positive. They wanted to work things out so that both of them felt comfortable.

A sense of humor is another essential personality trait to bring to a marriage. To be able to laugh at yourself and your eccentric mannerisms is to say, "I don't have to be perfect to be loved, and neither do you!"

If you spend your life with another person there are times when you feel irritable, and it is quite natural to turn that irritation on the other person. But one must have a sense of priorities in life. For example, let us say that Nadine wakes up one morning feeling a mild sense of anger which relates to nothing in reality. She walks into the kitchen and sees that Jason had left cigar butts overnight in an ashtray. He usually throws them out so as not to create an unpleasant odor but this time he had forgotten. Nadine's first response is "Damn him! Why doesn't he think!" Nadine already feels angry before she has encountered what is basically a mild irritation. Should she blow up when Jason enters the kitchen and enjoy letting off steam? That will, of course, make him feel bad. Or should she be understanding and forgiving, let it pass, and make an attempt to analyze why she felt angry in the first place?

You see by this example that a person has a choice to make regarding her own emotions. Nadine thought: "Why am I angry in the first place? Why should cigar butts become so important to me that I want to yell at my friend, lover, and husband?"

She sat down and began to free associate on her original feeling of anger. She thought: "Today is Tuesday—that means nothing—let's see—the date is November 9—what happened on that day? Oh God, it's my sister's birthday!" She remembered feeling mad at her mother for having another baby. That's where the angry feeling came from.

Remember, the repressed unconscious memories in all of us respond to everyday situations without conscious awareness of them. However, if you are willing to free associate you can discover the unconscious material.

In this case Nadine put Jason's feelings ahead of her wish to indulge in angry accusations. She chose to discover what was really going on internally. By the time Jason came into the kitchen she had regained her usual sense of well-being. "Good morning, cigar fiend!" she said. He laughed and replied, "It smells like hell in here— my fault!" They both laughed and the morning began in a state of friendly bantering.

Because Jason is a writer and Nadine an artist, they both work at home and, therefore, spend most of their lives together. They take coffee breaks together. Grocery shopping, the housework, and cooking are all shared endeavors. They are unusual in the sense that most married couples separate at eight in the morning and are together again at six or seven in the evening. The added pressure of living completely together is a true test of Jason and Nadine's relationship. Because they truly like each other as people as well as being very much in love, their circumstances please them.

Neither of them would dream of making rules for the other or of attempting to regulate the other's activities. If Nadine has plans with friends during the day, Jason feels happy for her. And Nadine does not suffer from jealously if Jason wants to be alone or go fishing with a friend or do whatever he pleases.

Jealousy is not love. It is a neurotic hate reaction, which sends out the message: You belong to me and you can't enjoy anything or anyone else but me. This reaction emanates directly from the childhood Oedipal period when the id-ridden child wants all of everything.

Pat's husband was employed in an office where his brother's wife also worked. Pat felt jealous because they saw each other all the time. She had the fantasy that her husband and his sister-in-law spent coffee breaks together and hours talking secretively. In reality they did no such thing. The office where they worked was very busy and they rarely spoke to one another.

In going back to Pat's childhood and questioning her about old feelings of being "left out," we discovered that this was how she felt when she was at school. She just knew that her mother and a preschool-age sister were doing special things—without her. Her jealous feeling of the present had nothing to do with her husband and his sister-in-law but came from her childhood. She had never resolved those childhood feelings. When Pat gained insight into why she was feeling jealous, she was able to give up her envy of her husband's relationships with other people.

Your marriage deserves much time and attention to make it into the most rewarding emotional experience of your life. Verbal communication about your needs and your feelings is essential. Not very many people are mind readers, so it is your responsibility to let your husband know how you feel.

There should be no masks worn in marriage. If either one or the other of a couple always tries to placate the other, or let one be "boss," then hostility builds up. Those hostile feelings soon may grow out of proportion to any actual event. It is much better to have a heated discussion than to smile your way through irritation and then bash up the car or drop a bowl of hot soup in your husband's lap—by accident, of course.

Many people say about their mate's family, "I'm marrying him, not his family!" Wrong. He is the product of his family. His conscious awareness grew from his experiences within his family. So you do marry the family, not just him. I've found that it is best for newly married people to move some distance from their parents if any of the parents is bossy or too nosy. Two people have a job to do in marriage and they do not need meddling parents to add unnecessary pressure to their new relationship. In the best circumstances, parents should be preoccupied with their own marriages and lives rather than with interfering with those of their children. It's wonderful if an enjoyable, equitable relationship can be established between the newly married and the older, more experienced generation.

A good rule to follow is to honor your parents if they are honorable people and love them if they deserve your love. It's nice to be able to call your mother or mother-in-law and ask some question, thus allowing her to share her life's experience with you. If she only wants to control your new family, though, or tries to put down your efforts, it is better to get your information elsewhere.

If you have been an independent person before deciding to marry, then you will not find running a household too difficult. That is another advantage of "getting it all together" before you invest your energies in a marriage. If both you and your prospective mate will work outside the home, it is only reasonable that both of you should share the household duties. But do not assume that everything will work out without some kind of planning. You must talk with your prospective mate about these things, and when talking, it is important that you both be completely honest with each other. Many people have the mistaken idea that they can change things, including their mate's attitudes, after the marriage. That is not true. If, for example, you are going with a compulsive gambler, marriage is not going to cure what is essentially a neurotic problem. The same is true of obesity, drunkenness, jealousy, controlling attitudes, and cruelty. Marriage is not some kind of magical occurrence that alters personalities.

If you feel irritated when your boyfriend watches football all day Sunday, do not misrepresent yourself and think that you will feel differently after the marriage. It is foolish to tell yourself, "I won't be angry after we're married, so I'll just pretend to not mind now."

If you are jealous of his sports interests now, it will only be compounded when you live together. You should ask yourself: "If I truly love and like him, why do I want to deprive him of his pleasure in watching football? Why should I want to spoil it for him?"

The passive watching of aggressive games has always been an excellent means of discharging aggression. Men enjoy games of physical power and skill. It has nothing to do with you. Would you consider that the time you spend in some hobby such as knitting, sewing, or painting takes away from your love for him?

Another question you should investigate if you feel jealous of anyone or anything your mate finds interesting is, "What would I rather that he be doing?" Frequently the answer to this question is, "Spending all of his time with me." That wish also goes back to your childhood id demand to have all of your parents' attention. If you explore the other implications of this answer, you might discover how unpleasant it would be to have another person give all of his attention to you. What about when you want to have a couple of private hours to yourself for writing letters, reading, or performing a beauty routine? Would you really enjoy having a man hovering over your every activity? The selfish child says, "I want all of your attention—but only when

I want it!" That is what you really mean when you say you want your mate to spend all of his time with you.

Jealous reactions remind me of the little boy who is happy and content playing with his blocks until the telephone rings and his mother answers it and begins a conversation. All of a sudden the little boy has a million things he must ask his mother. His questions are merely an attempt to get her attention, attention he neither needed nor wanted before her attention was directed toward another person.

The intense, angry feelings that are aroused in the early months of a marriage can be traced back to childhood. We bring into marriage all of our wishes for a family. If we did not receive love and kindness when we were children, we expect and demand it from our new family. You can again see how important it is to know your unconscious, your repetition pattern, and your hang-ups before you marry.

The unconscious, as you may have discovered, is quite clever in getting you to act out its wishes. One of the major complaints of newly married people is a sense of disappointment, of being cheated. Both people feel that their partner misrepresented himself. That is not really the case at all. The unconscious seems to give people a kind of vacation so that they can establish a relationship. It allows the individual to feel and act in all the loving ways he or she is capable of doing. All the tender and thoughtful attitudes that lovers feel and share with their prospective mates represent real feelings. However, when the emotional contact is fully established, the family unconscious wakes up and reasserts itself, and the old neurotic patterns emerge.

At this point in the marriage many couples begin to exist together in a spirit of resignation, not knowing that the qualities they fell in love with are real and still present. Those qualities are hiding behind the unconscious mechanism. It is at this time in the marriage relationship that the two people must genuinely work together to thwart and overcome their unconscious patterns. If they are willing to expend the effort, they will be able to regain the pleasure and excitement they originally found in each other. Because most people are unaware of the unconscious processes, they give in and seek to find this excitement instead in work, play, or another relationship.

One can hardly discuss marriage without mentioning divorce, as sometimes divorce is the only solution to a bad and unsalvageable marriage.

Frieda and Paul married while they were college students. Frieda was seventeen and Paul, a second-year medical student, was twenty-four. From the beginning of their life together theirs was a parent-child, bully-victim relationship. Frieda's father had died when she was thirteen, a very bad time for a girl, for it is during adolescence that she desperately needs her father and his validation of her personhood and femaleness.

In marriage Frieda was really seeking a father to replace the one she had lost, a man who would take care of her and tell her what to do. Paul was looking for someone whom he could dominate and who would make him feel important. His own family had always pushed him around because he was the youngest child and the only son in a family of four daughters. Since we do to others when we are grown what was done to us when we were children, Paul needed someone to "shove." Frieda and

Paul had a perfectly dovetailing neurotic match. He had found an infantile person to control and she had found a father image who would take care of everything.

Paul handled all money matters, from insurance forms to giving Frieda a daily allowance. He doled out her lunch and bus money each day, having convinced himself and her that she would lose the money if he gave it to her weekly or monthly. He purchased her clothes for her. He decided on their social life and he insisted that she agree with all his opinions. All this was fine with Frieda, as her unconscious wish to be taken care of was being satisfied. Moreover, since at seventeen one's identity is not established, she found it easy to be whatever he desired.

Paul wanted to have an "all-American girl" so he began to shape Frieda into his image. He had her grow long hair, wear clothes appropriate to that image, and change her manner of walking and talking. Even though their financial situation was rather tight, Paul budgeted enough money to send Frieda to a charm school. Quietly, under the surface of Frieda's passivity, however, there was a growing sense of herself as a person. This was taking place even as Paul continued to make his plans. He had decided that she should finish college so that she would be a well-educated doctor's wife. He directed her into acquiring a humanities degree as he reasoned that her studying a liberal arts curriculum would not pose a threat to him. But he had not reckoned on outside influences.

In her junior year, at the age of twenty, she was advised by her academic counselor to take a creative writing course to fill out her schedule. The instructor for the course was a well-known author who felt that anyone who wanted to write should not be confined to a specific form. He suggested that each student write a poem on any subject he wished and without worrying about style, form, or content. Frieda discovered that it was very easy for her to write poetry. While other students were agonizing over their first poetic endeavor, Frieda had written ten long poems. When she turned them in, the stunned teacher realized that he had a gifted artist on his hands. He started working with her. He gave her books to read and, in general, encouraged her talent. Soon she was publishing poetry and attracting the critical notice of various editors and readers. She was invited to give a reading of her poems on the campus.

Paul had paid little attention to her growing interest in poetry. She had shown her work to him, but he was not really interested and would usually say, "That's nice dear but I don't understand poetry." If asked, he would have said he thought it was "cute" that she had "taken up" poetry. However, when he attended her poetry reading, he could no longer ignore the fact that his possession was suddenly becoming an independent person. He discovered that his wife was an individual who was admired and respected on her own. The result of this episode was that when they arrived home, Paul had a hysterical reaction. He called her poems "communistic" and told her that she was never to write another one.

But one cannot frustrate a person's creative talents. A poet or a painter has to express himself and in his own way. At first Frieda was alarmed at what she felt was a drastic change in Paul whom she had always thought to be so understanding. What she now, realized was that

Paul was a kind person so long as he was in complete control of her thoughts, feelings, and actions. Frieda now began to see her relationship with Paul as it really was. The self-esteem she had developed through her writing and the recognition she had received allowed her to examine her marriage more closely. What was happening was that Frieda was growing up, as all emotionally healthy adolescents do.

She was now twenty years old and Paul was twenty-seven. At the time he married he had already gone through the process of identity solidification. Now he was still the same person, but Frieda was changing. Gradually their once peaceful master-servant relationship was destroyed. Frieda no longer wanted to be dictated to and she pleaded with him to let them live their life together as equal partners.

Paul suggested that they have a baby. He thought that their having a child would stop all this nonsense about Frieda being a person rather than "his" wife. To his surprise, Frieda refused but suggested that they seek treatment to resolve their differences.

When the marriage counselor pointed out Paul's need to be in control, Paul stormed out of the office in indignation. Frieda stayed and continued therapy for three months. Each day she became more herself. She still loved Paul, but she did not like the pattern of their relationship. She felt they could work out a mutual relationship of love and friendship if only he would see her as herself rather than as a mythical all-American girl-child whom he owned. But Paul refused to look at himself or his wife realistically or to change in any way. There was no solution but divorce.

When the subject of divorce came up, Paul ranted

and raved. He threatened to commit suicide and tried all kinds of emotional manipulation, but not once did he consider the possibility of changing his attitude toward Frieda. They were finally divorced.

Paul married soon afterward. His professional position was considered socially desirable, and he had no difficulty in finding a second wife. Because of his repetition compulsion to control someone else, he again chose a very immature girl. The process of creating the all-American girl image he wanted started all over again. His friends wondered how long it would take before his second wife grew up and left him and he would have to seek out another immature girl to work on. His was an easily recognizable pattern of behavior.

Frieda knew that she should live alone and be independent, thus she had accepted no alimony from Paul. She learned to take care of herself and soon became a whole person. At that point, she began to actively look for a partner to share her life.

Because the unconscious never changes in its intent (although we can change its effect on our lives), it is necessary to be alert to its demands. Frieda knew that her unconscious caused her to be attracted to controlling, paternal men. She would say, "If I'm immediately attracted to a man I think—oh no, that's my neurotic choice at work again. So let's look a little closer!" By being aware of her unconscious neurotic choice, she soon was able to avoid men who were the same type as Paul. She started giving other men a chance in her life. Finally she found and loved a man who was perfect for her. They have lived together for two years now and have a deep sense of happiness in their marriage.

We cannot blame either Frieda or Paul for their

choice of each other. Both of them were driven by their deep unconscious desires to be controlled and to control. Their marriage would have been successful if Frieda had never grown up. It still would have been a neurotic match, but a working one.

Although a divorce is a blow to one's ego, it should be looked upon as a means of rectifying a mistake and the beginning of an effort not to make the same kind of mistake again.

But many people, like Paul, do make the same error the second time around. That happens when the person has no insight into his unconscious motivations. If you get a divorce, you owe it to yourself to discover and understand your neurotic mate choice. Only in that way will you be able to avoid repeating your original error.

To sum it all up—a happy, fulfilled married life is possible. In order to achieve it, however, you must bring to your marriage a strong sense of self-esteem, the ability to be a true friend, and a willingness to be open in expressing all feelings, negative as well as positive. Further, it is essential to have a desire for a lifelong partnership and the ability to love without infantile demands or infantile dependency. Those are the qualities of a mature genital personality.

Indeed, your system of personal ethics should require that you not seek a marriage partner until you consider yourself a genital person. If you demand the best emotional level for your own life, you have the right to demand the same qualities in your partner.

VIII.

BECOMING
A PARENT

It is only in the last decade that women have been given the opportunity to realistically appraise their life situation before becoming pregnant. In the past it was assumed that when people married they would naturally have children. Economic reasons, as well as the logical concept that the purpose of marriage was procreation, lent strength to that assumption.

Now the threat of overpopulation is regarded as a serious danger to the availability of adequate living space, to reasonable consumption of our natural resources, and to control of the varied forms of pollution. In addition, for personal or economic reasons, more and more young people are choosing either not to have children or to limit their families to one or two children. And in 1973 the Supreme Court ruled that within certain limitations based on medical reasons, a woman who wishes to have an abortion is free to do so. With the ready availability of contraceptive devices, however, unwanted pregnancies should rarely have to occur.

There is a biological drive in the female to produce children. Female bodies are regulated to the function of creation, as they are equipped with eggs, a womb, and the ability to produce milk. But even though the human body has changed little from the beginning of human time, society has changed significantly. Becoming a parent is now considered something that should be carefully thought over in advance by both partners rather than simply being allowed to occur by chance.

By the time you have read this far, you will have been impressed by the complexity of human relationships and the complicated and delicate process of physical and psychological growth. So, if you are considering pregnancy, you must think far beyond the romantic joys of having a baby to the facts of actually rearing a child from infancy through adolescence. Being a parent is one of the most awesome and responsible jobs of any person's life. It is not to be undertaken lightly. We have seen how much time, energy, and insight must be devoted to establishing a deeply meaningful relationship in marriage. It seems only fair that you should not bring another individual into that union unless you have worked out and have lived a satisfying relationship for some time.

If you are not mature yourself, you should not consider foisting your immaturity onto a helpless infant who needs constant and responsible attention. It is very important to keep in mind these facts: The birth of a child never accomplished any of the following:

1. Saved a marriage.
2. Brought the parents permanently closer together.
3. Resolved neurotic problems.
4. Kept a roving mate at home.

The above are some of the reasons often given for having children. These reasons are based on faulty, immaturely thought out premises. It is not reasonable to expect the birth or presence of an infant to resolve the parents' emotional conflicts.

The only acceptable time for bringing another human being into a marriage is when the husband and wife deeply love one another and feel that they are mature genital people. They must want to give life to another person. They also must recognize that all of the love, labor, time, and expense involved in rearing that child will be their responsibility.

They have to realize, too, that the child will be with them only for the time he needs to go through his growth process. When the child develops his own resources and becomes an independent person, he will leave home and make his own life. Prospective parents should not feel that they are going to *own* a child. After giving a child life, their main purpose is to care and guide him toward his own autonomy.

If you believe that by having a child, you will have someone to take care of you in your old age, then you will be disappointed. That is no longer the custom in our culture. Expecting your child to take care of you means that you have not grown up yourself, that you still have a basically dependent personality. You will have to go back three steps and start again.

The only reward effective, loving parents should expect is the knowledge of a life's job done well. Parents owe the child they conceived and birthed the best upbringing they are emotionally capable of giving. A child does not owe his parents thanks for having done their job successfully.

If after eighteen years of parenthood you find that

your independent offspring is willing and able to have a mutually respectful and loving relationship with you, that in itself should be all the thanks you need.

So before you rush into parenthood, consider honestly why you want to have children. Ask yourself also what you expect to give to them and receive in return. Allow yourself to freely associate on these questions and carefully examine your motivations.

Consider, too, your role as a mother. In our discussion of the growth of the ego and superego, you have seen how essential it is for the mother to be the person who takes care of the child. The infant and the toddler has a physical and an emotional need for his mother, and if you do not wish to take on this responsibility, you really should not have children. A child is not helped if someone else does the vital job of mothering.

Further, you should not assume that because you want to have a baby that your husband does too. If you are honest with each other that, of course, will not occur. But it is important to remember that you cannot force another person to want to be a parent until he is emotionally ready. Fooling a man and accidentally becoming pregnant will only make him feel he has been trapped. He will naturally feel hostile, and both you and the baby will suffer the effects of that hostility perhaps for many years.

Therefore the decision to begin to add to your existing family of two must be by mutual agreement because, as you know from our discussion of the development of personality structure, a child needs *two* attentive and responsible parents. Some couples decide that they simply do not wish to have children. In realistically evaluating their relationship and their individual and combined life goals, they find that they receive so much satisfaction from living and loving together that they honestly do not want to invest their time, love, and energy in children. That attitude is perfectly acceptable, particularly in light of today's social and population problems. Indeed, it should have been acceptable in the past, but until now people were "programmed" differently.

If you and your mate have mutually decided to have a child together, and if your decision has been based on a sound marital situation, the months of pregnancy should be a delightful time of life. Pregnancy is not illness. Many women who suffer from "morning sickness" are unconsciously trying to throw up the baby because a part of them does not really want the child. If you do have these symptoms, you should use the techniques of self-analysis. By being honest with yourself and engaging in free association you can rid yourself of them.

When you become pregnant, you should immediately choose an obstetrician with whom you feel comfortable. He will answer your questions and give you dietary advice so that you can maintain a healthy body during your pregnancy.

When you love your man, there is a delightful feeling of sharing in the process of creation which is going on inside of your body. Loved and loving women when pregnant literally glow with health and happiness.

Sometimes men worry during their wives' pregnancy that when the baby comes, their wives will turn all of their love on the child. If your husband has any such fears he should be able to talk to you openly about them. You should be able to explain that your genital love relationship with him is an entirely different kind of love from that which a mother feels for a child. It is true that nature has left men out of the process of creation except for the act of intercourse. A man can never have the experience of life growing and moving inside of him. No body changes prepare him for the coming role of parenthood. In order to help her husband to feel a major part of the pregnancy, a woman should try to share her feelings and experiences with him.

Years ago during my training to become a psychoanalyst, I worked in a natural childbirth clinic which was operated by nurse-midwives of the Medical Missionary Sisters. One of our foremost concerns was to make the pregnancy and birth experience a family affair. We had classes for both the prospective mother and father which included such things as prenatal exercises, the joys of breast-feeding, and the emotional states of both parents. Even among couples who were unmarried, the fathers-to-be were included.

The men came to the classes regularly and got very involved in the creative process. We encouraged the fathers to be present during labor and the birth of their child. Their emotional support and presence during delivery was of great help to their wives and sweethearts. Often the women asked their men to just hold their hands as they worked to have their babies.

When a child was born, the nun who was the midwife in charge of the delivery always held the infant toward the father and asked him to bless his new child into the world. It was a simple love ritual whereby each man gave his own blessing, whether he was Catholic, of another faith, or an atheist. Some men made the sign of the cross over the child's head; others kissed the infant's forehead. I remember one young hippie father who had a bell to ring and some pure mountain stream water with which to touch the baby. Tears of love were always shed by those of us who were present at the beginning of a new family. Here were mother, father, and child all participating in the ageless miracle of birth.

If more people insisted on a family situation during pregnancy and delivery, institutions and doctors would have to change their attitude toward the father. They would stop shunting him off to waiting rooms as if he had no right to participate in this important event in his life.

I once knew a man who was so frustrated by the doctor and the hospital that he handcuffed himself to his wife during her labor. It was only his drastic action that made it possible for him to share his wife's experience of giving birth. That should not be necessary. Adults should not be treated by institutions as if they were helpless children. Rules should be changed to permit a family to remain together at this crucial time.

Genital men find the body of a pregnant woman very beautiful. They are not offended by the sight of the growing womb. If a man is or thinks he might be offended by this change in his woman, his feelings should be discussed. If you, the woman, feel offended by yourself you should examine your self-esteem.

During your pregnancy you should consider the joys of breast-feeding. Before feeding bottles were developed, women nursed their infants as a matter of course, because their milk was obviously for that purpose. For those few babies whose mothers were physically unable to nurse them, a substitute mother, or wet nurse, was provided whose job it was to provide milk for the baby. It was only after the invention of the baby bottle that many women suddenly discovered that they "just couldn't nurse." The fact is, however, there are really very few women incapable of nurturing their babies as nature intended.

In the baby's oral stage of development he requires a sense of closeness to the mother. When nursing a baby you fulfill all of the basic needs in his life and begin his ego growth with a love bond that will remain deep in his unconscious all of his life.

In nursing, the baby is held next to your body and he feels its natural warmth. He feels your heartbeat, too, and its stable rhythm gives him a sense of security. A child knows his mother's smell and his nose resting against your breast reassures him and makes him feel comfortable. Breast-feeding also allows the infant to have the amount of the sucking he needs, as there is always a trickle of milk coming through the nipple. The more he sucks, the more milk is produced so that supply satisfies the demand in a very natrual way. Because babies are not born with patience, they cannot and should not have to tolerate frustration. Breast-feeding eliminates this anxiety-producing emotion since you, the mother, are always ready with the supply of milk.

It is a beautiful, sensual experience to nurse a child. It adds to your self-esteem that you are able to maintain a life through your own body. You are also giving along with your body's milk a sense of love and trust to your child. When the baby begins to be able to see, his position at the breast allows him to focus his eyes on yours. You can actually begin to see his sense of love grow and develop.

Mothers often have sexual feelings when nursing their baby. They should be enjoyed as a pleasurable love feeling, for they are very normal and natural. They are just another of nature's ways to bind you closely with your child.

Breast-feeding also has practical benefits for the mother. It stimulates the uterus to mildly contract and thus you regain your shape much faster. And breast cancer is more rare in women who have nursed their babies.

A few months before you give birth you should arrange for a pediatrician to care for your baby's physical needs, and if you plan on nursing your baby, you should select the doctor carefully. If you have a La Leche League in your community, consult them as to who the doctors are who encourage breast-feeding.

You see, there is a peculiar attitude prevalent in our society. Breast-feeding, a normal and natural process, has become unusual and is therefore deemed unnatural. Many nurses on obstetrical services are notorious for discouraging women from nursing their babies. They say it upsets their routine to have to bring the nursing child to the mother at night. So, instead of validating the mother for doing the healthiest thing, both physically and mentally, for herself and her baby, they try to instill doubt about the process of breast-feeding. They say, "Are you sure that you have enough milk?" or "Oh my, the baby isn't gaining strength!" These are remarks calculated to create a sense of anxiety in the mother so that she will give up and let the nurses bottle-feed her baby and keep their routines in order. Do not listen to them.

Some doctors use the same techniques, so you must avoid them. Other mothers and female relatives, many of whom feel envious of your close relationship with your nursing baby, will try to put you down with similar remarks. If you understand their jealous manipulations for what they are, you will not be bothered by their intrusive attitude.

Breast-fed babies do not gain weight as quickly as bottle-fed babies, but that is quite natural. Babies are intended to gain slowly and not blow up like balloons from cow's milk. At first breast-fed infants feed every two and one half to three hours, not because they are not getting enough milk but because that is how their bodies are regulated. Further, their bowel movements do not smell as bad when they are breast-fed as when they are on cow's milk. They sleep better and are usually more content than bottle-fed babies.

Babies who are breast-fed also receive natural antibodies against disease through the mother's milk. In general, they rarely suffer from colic or spitting up.

The best people to have in your life when you are nursing are a loving, proud father who shares your attitude about giving your child the best physical and emotional start in life, a supportive pediatrician, and a good friend. Your good friend, whether she is a relative or some other woman, should be one who has nursed her children and loved it.

Some of the rationalizations I have heard for not nursing deserve attention, if only to point out their faulty reasoning. One is, "It's like an animal!" Well, we happen to be animals, of the mammal classification. Mammals nurse their young. You may say that you do not like being put in that category, but it is a biological fact. For that reason, nature provides you with the milk to nurture your young. Do you really want to withhold your infant's right to his natural food?

Two, "It ties you down!" If you expect to run around and do all of the things you did in the past, then why have a baby in the first place? A baby needs his mother a great deal of the time anyway, so how can nursing be the one factor that ties you down? It takes only about thirty minutes to complete the nursing period every three or four hours. How many times are you going to be away from your home for three or four hours without your baby? In fact, nursing mothers can find a place to feed their babies almost anywhere, and they do not have to be bothered with taking along bottles and formulas. It is actually easier with a breast-fed baby to go places then it is with a bottle-fed baby.

Three, "It will ruin my figure!" It does not ruin your figure to nurse, anymore than pregnancy ruins your figure. It is up to you to get back your original shape and to keep yourself slim and your muscle tone good. Breast-feeding has no adverse effect on the figure.

Four, "I'd never know if the baby has had enough!" Everything does not have to be measured in ounces. You can tell when the baby has had enough because when he is satisfied he falls asleep at the breast.

Five, "It's too much trouble!" It's no trouble because the milk is always there and at the right temperature. There are no bottles to sterilize. There is no formula to buy and prepare. And, as I pointed out earlier, it's easier to take a breast-fed baby with you than to have to take baby plus all of his feeding paraphernalia.

I consider it very important to give the child this oral experience. The close body contact will provide an excellent start to the growth of a loving, trusting, and secure person. Thus you have the opportunity to allow your child to grow a strong ego from the beginning of his life. It involves approximately ten months of giving on your part and yet the rewards continue for the remainder of your child's existence. Breast-fed babies usually wean themselves and are on a cup by the age of one year. Whereas bottle-fed babies, because their experience is not as satisfying, hang on much longer to their bottles. Indeed, bottle-feeding creates fixations.

If you have psychological reasons for not wanting to nurse your infant, I recommend you try to overcome them for the sake of your child and his normal development. If you are one of the few women who are physically unable to nurse, then make sure that you always hold your infant when feeding him. Place his cheek against your warm breast and give him his bottle that way.

Propping the baby and his bottle up and leaving the child alone while he feeds is cruel. It makes him relate to a thing, "the bottle," rather than to a person. It creates serious adult oral problems. And, if you have to leave your baby, make sure the baby-sitter is a kind and loving person who will carry through on providing a sense of security for your emotionally fragile infant.

Throughout your pregnancy, you will probably wonder what the baby will look like and whether it will be a boy or a girl. However, if you feel strongly that you must have a child of a specific sex, you should analyze that desire. It should be a child that you want, not a boy or a girl. Remember that an infant picks up your feelings toward it and if you are disappointed over its sex, he or she will know it. A sense of not being the right one will grow in his unconscious.

If you feel an urgency to have a son, find out your unconscious reasons and deal with them before the child's birth. Some women who feel inferior as females have a great desire to produce a boy. These women feel that they will have finally achieved their maleness by having a son. This is neurotic thinking and will interfere with the development of the child who is born, whether son or daughter.

For your sake, therefore, and the sake of the child you have invited into the world, clear up your emotional clutter about infant sex choice so that you can love whoever is born.

There has been a great deal of nonsense communicated to women about the awful pain of childbirth and adding to the idea of childbearing as an infirmity rather than a natural phenomena. In many women fear and anxiety cause more pain than is necessary. The labor and delivery process are the body's mechanism to allow birth to take place. If you are wise enough to follow a supervised exercise program during pregnancy, you will be able to help your body deliver your child. That is better than allowing yourself to be anesthetized out of a beautiful and exciting experience. Many doctors and nurses prefer the delivering mother to be unconscious simply for the efficiency of their established routines, ignoring the fact that a baby born while the mother is under heavy sedation is also sedated.

Labor and delivery are nothing to fear if they take place within the emotional context of having a wanted child as a symbol of mutual love.

When labor begins, the contractions are felt as a pressure which grows in intensity as your cervix dilates in order to permit the infant to pass through to be born. The pain is unlike any other you will ever experience. But most other pains in life have no reward except that they eventually cease. However, there is a reward for the pressure and pain in childbirth in that your body has worked to help your striving child into the world. A loved woman senses a spiritual elevation of the creative force that carries her beyond the physical experience and discomfort.

If you insist, the doctor will allow you to watch in a mirror as your child comes out of your body. There is nothing in life to compare with the glory of this visual experience. You, working with your body, the baby striving to be born, and suddenly the head appears, then the face, arms, body, legs—your child!

Since you are conscious, you can see your baby immediately and hold it in your arms with the man you love by your side. The sense of being a mother and deeply involved in this child's birth with your mate beside you is truly exquisite.

The pain you have experienced dissolves in your memory as soon as the baby is born. Birth is a glorious and unique life adventure that should not be missed. Do not be a passive body that allows science and hospital routine to rob you of this elemental and joyful experience.

After delivery you will be tired. You should have nothing external to worry about, which is the reason you will have made all of your preparations before the birth. You will have arranged for a pediatrician, proper clothing for the infant, a crib, and other needed items. You should also have arranged for your mother, a friend, relative, or paid help to be ready to help you out at home for at least two weeks after you and the baby leave the hospital.

It is also a good idea for you to have laid in grocery supplies and perhaps have cooked several main dishes ahead and frozen them for use when you come home. It is important that these everyday tasks do not impinge upon the primary responsibility of your new family situation.

Your main job will be to regain your strength after the physical exertion of delivery and to nurse the baby. Your milk is not fully available for approximately three to four days after delivery. It usually comes in suddenly, however, and the baby, often on the first day home, seems to want to nurse for a few minutes at each breast, at least once every hour. That is nature's way of stimulating milk production and does not mean that you are not satisfying the child's nutritional needs. Be sure to drink plenty of fluids—water, milk, juices, beer—to help your body produce milk. If you have made adequate plans for a helper to do all the other things, you can rest in bed with the baby right beside you, napping and nursing.

There should absolutely be *no* company except your husband for the first two days. You do not need to entertain relatives, friends, and neighbors. You are recuperating, and your sense of serenity and the baby's needs come first. This should be thoroughly discussed with your husband beforehand so that he understands and does not feel excluded.

You may feel a sudden sense of vulnerability to the world when you leave the hospital and may feel, for no apparent reason, tearful. Everyone regresses to some extent when he is in a hospital, so the less time spent there the better. As long as you have made plans for peace and quiet, you will regain your feelings of adulthood after a day or two at home. These feelings are not related to breast-feeding as some people might want you to believe.

Depending upon your personal physical make-up, your stitches will soon disappear. Warm baths, lots of them, will really help.

Babies quickly establish a three- or four-hour sleeping pattern between feedings and a routine will develop. Most babies seem to spend some time during the day or night being irritable. Again, this is not related to breast-feeding. A comfortable rocking chair is a boon to the mother and child. You can gently rock yourself and the child during this period or your husband may wish to rock the baby. It really is not fair, however, to expect him to get up in the middle of the night if he has to go to work early the next morning. You can nap with the baby during the day and he cannot. If you and your husband have established a sharing love relationship before your child is born, then he is not going to feel "used" if he helps out with the bathing and changing of the baby when he is at home. But he cannot nurse or give the cuddling a mother can, so you should not expect him to take over your mothering responsibilities.

Many women feel upset if they have aggressive or sexual fantasies about their infants. But that is usual and normal, and as long as you do not act them out, there is nothing to feel guilty about. As I stated before, we do to others what was done to us. You can break this chain of events, however. Battered children have parents who were brutalized themselves. If you find yourself irritated at your helpless child, then examine your feelings with complete honesty, understand their origins, and accept them as being part of your make-up. Talk to your husband or to another mother if you have difficulty in coping with your feelings.

Remember the deep influence the mother has on the child's ego and superego. You will see your infant grow into the toddler and anal stage and then on toward the phallic and Oedipal periods and be able to help him grow. You are a vital person in his psychosexual development during the oral and anal stages. The father's importance becomes more profound when children enter the phallic period. That is not to say that he should absent himself until that time. On the contrary, your relationship together, your sense of mutual love and respect, will flow into the infant's perceptive apparatus and he will begin to know that this is how a family should be.

I do not mean to give the impression that the mother must be chained to her infant. After all, he sleeps a great deal of the time and you deserve your time away from him and the house. I am speaking of the emotional qualities a mother owes her growing child.

Your role as a mother changes throughout a child's life. When he is an infant, he needs and is entitled to much fondling, cuddling, kissing, and nursing. If you give him an abundance of warmth and love during infancy, he will not be a clinging child always in search of that which he was deprived of during babyhood.

When the child is going through the superego growth, your role changes. As the child's ego tries to control his id desires, you become the giver of earned love.

During the phallic and Oedipal development you are a gentle frustrater who pushes the child into a relationship with the waiting father. You must give up being the most important person in your child's existence and allow him to establish feelings for others.

Your role changes again when the child enters society and attends school. He will have his secrets and his pals and will not include you. You are still needed, but your child should no longer be emotionally dependent upon you.

The most emotionally demanding time for mothers is during the period of adolescent turmoil. This is when the person who is no longer a child and not yet an adult needs guidance without bullying. He needs love without suffocation, acceptance without patronization, and advice without lecturing. Most of all, the mother must let the child become himself, make his own mistakes, and have his victories with a growing sense of independence.

I have not elaborated upon the physical duties of parenthood because there are so many books available on the subject. My main concern is for the parent to understand the emotional investment required in good parenthood.

IX.

ROMANCE IS NOT A SOMETIME THING

Isn't it interesting how much time, money, and creative talent are spent in this country selling the idea of romance? Children are bombarded from their first television viewing with advertisements that impliedly promise eternal romance if one only purchases a particular automobile, an underarm shaver, or a certain brand of soap. On television the resulting romantic matches seem so smooth and pleasant—no one ever stutters, leaves crumbs on his face, or gets exhausted.

In puberty and adolescence, girls can dream and drool over teen-age romance magazines, graduating to such as *True Love*, *Real Romance*, and *Movie Life*. Men's magazines extol the good life with gorgeous women hanging on the "with it" male who is dressed in the latest high fashion. Because children are gullible, they really do believe those glossy pictures of their favorite movie, television, and singing stars in their impeccable clothing, living and playing in luxurious surroundings, their children and spouses equally tidy and lovable. Husbands and wives are shown gazing adoringly at each other while their children look worshipfully into their eyes.

The readers, impressionable youngsters, would be shocked to see the reality behind the images—that the house is a "set" and that an army of personnel was required to get everyone dressed, coiffed, and made-up perfectly and in their places at the right time. That the people are posed and the camera angles arranged to show the subjects to their best advantage. But the naive audience believes that these pictures represent reality. And they assume that the same lucky fate is due them as privileged Americans who use all the right commercial products.

Romantic ballads also play a part in forming the young person's expectations of his future rewards. Everyday he can hear dozens of songs that promise him that there is no limit to love and no unpleasantness in romance.

Why is it, then, that people see so little of this promised love and romance around them? Most kids look at their parents and other adults and wonder where the romance is. Try as hard as they may, they do not seek a speck of romance in those adult lives, even though their parents looked at the same romantic advertisements and listened to the same types of love songs as they themselves do now. It is as if people over thirty had ceased to dream.

Adults encourage young people to believe that romance does not exist in adulthood. As they moon over their romantic heroes and heroines, whether they be movie stars, sports personalities, popular singers, or their own contemporaries on whom they have crushes, they are told: "What you feel is puppy love, it won't last!"

178

or "Enjoy yourself now while you can have romantic ideas, but just wait until you're an adult and you'll find that life is different!" This version of reality is at complete variance with messages they have received since childhood from television and the magazines. What has gone wrong? Who is right and who is wrong?

Looking realistically at the media portrayal of life and romance reveals several discrepancies which destroy its applicability to real-life situations. Most of the stories, movies, commercials, and advertisements that depict romantic situations portray the people in them as handsome and beautiful. But the situations themselves are not real and in the case of films and advertising the people who play the roles make their living because of their good looks. In real life, such people are rather rare.

All the promises of lasting romance are an appeal to the id in all of us that wants everything without having to work for it. That is why we like to see the depiction of the romantic ideal in plays, television, advertising, and stories. In these fictitious renderings of life, the happy couple is sprinkled with romance and all the other good things of life. All they have to do is stand still for this magic shower and from then on romance becomes a part of their lives "forever." The id in all of us responds to this message, because it represents getting something for nothing.

These examples of romance have no quality of realism. As with the movie star's family portrait, everything is clean, neat, and in perfect order—a world without dirt, anxieties, death, or any of the other everyday facts of life. Romance is equated with a sterile sense of perfection.

When normal young people who have been fed all of this nonsense try to satisfy their longing for similar romance, trouble develops. Trying to fit these images of what romance should be into their own lives and particularly into a marriage is like trying to put together a jigsaw puzzle with all the wrong pieces. Reality is thus frustrating for them and husband and wife feel a deep sense of disappointment. Their marriage seems dull and colorless compared to what they have been led to expect from it. So they put aside that "silly nonsense" and get down to the business of getting through life. They give up on one of life's most rewarding emotions—a sense of daily romance with one's mate.

Emotional needs are a part of our psychological make-up. We all have deeply rooted needs for love and affection, and romance symbolizes these emotions.

The most uncontrollable need for love is present at birth when we are in a state of id control. Wanting love and expecting to give nothing in return is normal for the oral infant, but it is abnormal for the adult. However, the people who plan advertising understand very well that we all still have that id desire for love and romance that we do not have to work for. The advertiser's interest is in exploiting that desire. Remember that these hucksters of romance are trying to sell you, the consumer, a product whether it is a car, a new pop music star, or a deodorant. If they can convince you to buy their product because you believe the fiction they surround it with, that's not their responsibility. And if you are disappointed that their product does not change your life into something sparkling—that's your fault, not theirs. Their only job is to sell you.

The romantic urges that are manipulated by advertisers and the media are very real. However, knowledge of the ways in which a person can really achieve romance is withheld. Everyone, especially young people, should learn that romantic love is possible for all their lives but not on an "id basis."

It is a role of the ego to want to share love and romance with another and a superego task to say, "You can have it if you work for it." Your superego must tell you that, "Yes, you deserve romance and love but only if you are willing to give it in return." In other words, something for something, not something for nothing.

When two people fall in love with each other, all the stored-up longings for an adult love relationship engulf both of you in a glow of romantic feelings. These feelings are exciting and they embody the complete spectrum of all adolescent fantasies. At last, all of your romantic dreams have come true. You long to spend as much time as possible with each other. Every time you look into each other's eyes it is as if the other's soul is revealed with all of its longings and needs. You seek to find special ways of expressing your love. Whenever possible, each of you lets your loved one know how dear he or she is to you. You glance at each other, touch, telephone, or write, and think of a thousand other ways of conveying your feelings.

During courtship the feelings of high romance are real—one cannot manufacture feelings. Because their emotions are so overwhelming, however, the couple who have grown up with television, romantic stories, and advertising are likely to assume that they are finally getting what the media have promised. But if the feelings are genuine, they are not "received." Rather they come out of yourself and your needs to love and be loved. And if you are willing to put forth the effort to maintain and nourish it, romance can grow and flourish all of your life. It's just like anything else in life; you must earn your way in a mature genital fashion if you expect the rewards that make life precious.

Before you set up a home together, the time you spend with each other is usually freed of most of life's more mundane concerns. You come together with only the intent of being with each other. But how does one retain romance when you have the responsibilities of a home, whether it is an apartment, a trailer, a tent, or a house? Suddenly there are bills to pay, food shopping to be done, meals to cook, dirty dishes and dirty clothes to wash, unmade beds, and seemingly hundreds of other day-to-day chores to be done. With children, there are still more "reality oriented" tasks that have to be performed each day. In these circumstances, how can one keep romance alive and well?

It is not really that difficult, once you accept the fact that romance does not grow by itself like a sturdy weed, but is more like a delicate plant that needs careful attention from two adult people.

One factor that hinders romance is the unconscious. It can start burrowing a destructive path into your relationship even if you have made a suitable mate choice. That should not happen if you already understand your unconscious and its repetition compulsion. But if your unconscious makes you act pregenital, you may come to believe that the romantic love associated with your courtship was somehow unreal and is now best forgotten.

That is not true. Those loving romantic feelings were a measure of what the two of you are emotionally capable of giving each other, and they need not die. They can be made to live as an integral part of your daily life together.

To begin with the daily chores that people must attend to, a good rule is: just get them done. They do not have to be exaggerated in importance and made to loom too large in your life. Learn to simplify your life so that you do not have a thousand insignificant things to do. Keeping a clean home does not take all day. Everything does not have to be shining and spotless at all times. The soap and wax "pushers" would have you believe that scrubbing, washing, waxing, and polishing are the most valid tasks of everyday living. You should have learned in your days of living independently how to handle chores with dispatch. If you did not, then learn now and be done with it.

The emotional tone of the home is set by the woman. That is because during our first years we are dependent on our mothers, and whether we are male or female, she sets our individual emotional tones. That experience carries over into a male's adult life even though he may not be consciously aware of it. Consequently the man ordinarily waits to discern the woman's emotional and behavioral patterns in their home before asserting himself. As a woman, therefore, you have the opportunity to set the stage for pleasant romantic overtones in your life.

Of course the intensely romantic urgency you experienced when you first fell in love is going to smooth out, for it is difficult to maintain any emotion at a high pitch. Over a period of years a serene love feeling is more com-

fortable than a wild excitement. But romance is dependent on a couple's ability to convey how much they really
care for each other. Again, the media imply that this
means clutching embraces and the giving of expensive
gifts. Of course you will want to enjoy those deep linger-
ing soul kisses when you celebrate your feelings by making love, but the truth is that we cannot spend all of our
time in bed, even if we wanted to. And the best gifts are
romantic gestures. A smile that tells how happy you are
to wake up with this particular person beside you is like
the sun shining into the bedroom, whether you live in a
cold-water flat or a mansion.

The many ways of showing affection are life-giving
to romance. They are like food. A caress or a touch
while one or the other is doing some chore makes anyone feel special. To never unnecessarily let a loving
thought go unspoken is the commandment of romance.
This can be "How handsome you look!" "I love you,"
"Thank you," "You make me feel good," or anything
that pops into your mind. The moment for speaking
loving words is whenever they occur to you and will
not embarrass the other person. You do not say, "You
have the dearest dimples" when a man is trying to talk
on the telephone. That's being jealous and interfering
like an Oedipal child.

If your unconscious voices promise that you will be
laughed at or rejected if you utter endearing words,
then go back into your past and see when it happened
to you before. The irrational unconscious promise is
that you will be safer if you withhold love words from
another person who needs and deserves them. That is
another example of the nonsense that comes out of the

unconscious. You are now living your only life, so do not let love thoughts fade away unspoken.

Watching for and meeting your mate's needs is romantic. Maybe he feels really loved and special when you serve him coffee in bed—it's not hard to do and the next thing you know you may be in there with him. It's the unexpected that keeps a romance alive.

Candles and their soft glow symbolize romance, but you do not need a ten-foot-long table with crystal and fine china to use them. But neither should you set yourself up for rejection by putting candles on the dinner table when you know that he feels unhappy about something important, or that after dinner he has to study or go out. We all know intuitively how our mates are feeling and it is both romantic and common sense to pay attention and respond to those signals. It is another way of saying, "I love you and care about your feelings."

These remarks are not addressed only to the woman in the relationship, because small acts of concern and thoughtfulness must be a part of a mutual giving and receiving. All of these expressions of love take no real time, no great planning, and, unlike in movies, no orchestra music. Concern is all that is needed to show love. And without demonstration of love, everyday life becomes just existence.

Sometimes you cannot give all the love you might wish to give. There are times when it seems too difficult. We all get colds and the flu now and then, and when a person is sick he regresses and feels like a child. He wants to be taken care of. Both partners should understand that and be willing to temporarily set aside their own needs and give some mothering to the ill partner.

Indeed it makes a genital person feel good to occasionally take care of someone he loves. And when the ill person recovers, he or she should be able to resume the mutual give-and-take of a genital relationship

Children do not have to prevent romance. In fact the gestures that convey love and care should be evident to your children from infancy to adulthood. That will establish in their unconscious process the need for romantic love feelings in their own adult lives. What better legacy could you pass on to the future generation than this example of the daily living of a loving life?

However, parents should be able to spend some time away from their children. I do not believe that the hysterical child orientation in this country is good for children. They have their own world and it should be somewhat separated from the adult world. If you and your husband want a quiet time together when he or both of you come home from work, you can teach your children to respect your privacy. It will give them something to aspire to when they are adults. For example, children do not have to have dinner with you all the time. You can feed them and postpone your own dinner until after their bedtime. Eating alone with your husband gives the two of you a better chance to share each other's presence. If you want a vacation from the demands of children, take it and luxuriate in being alone with each other. You deserve it. Remember that common sense is still the best guideline in rearing children—no book can ever do the job for you.

Psychoanalysts have long been known for making lofty observations and proclamations about human behavior. And they have hidden their private lives as if it were necessary that there be some great mystery about them. However, we are just people like everybody else. We do have specialized training, but we still have the same emotional needs as others do.

I could not have written this book unless I felt that I had attained a state of genitality myself. It would have been vastly unfair to hold up the promise of a loving life if I did not know that it could, in fact, be achieved.

Recently my husband, who is also a psychoanalyst, was being interviewed on a television talk program. The television host queried him as to how he and his wife managed to get along. He asked him if it was not true that we were always analyzing each other. My husband said: "No, we're just like other people you know. After seeing our patients, we love to be together, have a drink, watch television, or talk. We really love each other very much." The interviewer looked quite surprised, and the technician in the control room where I was sitting turned to me and asked incredulously, "Is that really true?" I laughed and nodded my head.

We have three children and have been deeply in love for fourteen years. During this time our romantic and love feelings have grown and matured along with us. Our love is the center of our lives and is a constant source of sustenance to us.

Sigmund Freud once said that being analyzed helped a person to cope with the everyday miseries of life. Perhaps that was as much as one could expect in his day. We have discovered that when you overcome neurosis and establish a deep and binding love in life, then there are very few "everyday miseries." There are, naturally, external annoyances that cannot be avoided, but they really are of little consequence.

My husband and I were neurotic people at one time,

locked into our individual repetition compulsions. We were analyzed and grew into genital people who base our lives on our love. We did not come from wealth or special circumstances; we were just two people who strove to turn our lives into an adventure of living and loving. If we were able to do that, you can do it too. And if you can do it, so can your children.

That's what it's all about. To be able to love yourself, other people, and one special person, and to pass that "life formula" on to the next generation. It is based on the acceptance of emotional work as the price for the only rewarding emotion that man comes equipped with.

Use your brain, use your intuition, use your knowledge gained about the personality development of the female, and you can truly become a full and beautiful female being.

Index

Index

anal phase and, 40-46
breast-feeding and, 165-67, 170
oral phase and, 36-37, 74-75
phallic phase and, 48-53
See also Parent-child relationship

Narcissism, 80-82
Natural childbirth, 164-65, 171-72
Neurotic choice, 104, 145
marriage and, 157-58
Nursing, *see* Breast-feeding

Obesity, 31, 32
oral phase and, 74-75
Oedipal period, 48-53, 148, 175, 176
adolescence and, 57-58, 63, 65
father's power in, 129, 133-34, 143-44, 153
lesbianism and, 82, 85-87, 90
of male, 48-51
O'Keeffe, Georgia, 12
Oral phase of psychosexual development, 36-41, 55, 175
alcoholism and, 67-74
breast-feeding and, 37-39, 166, 170
narcissism and, 80-82
overindulgence in, 74-75, 78-79
Orgasm, 118-35
clitoral, 122, 123-24, 126-27
fear of, 130-32, 133-35
frigidity and, 119-20
male and female contrasted, 18, 118
pretension of, 130-32
vaginal, 126-29, 132-33
Ovary, 26
menstruation and, 27-29
Overpopulation, 159

Parent-child relationship, 11, 94-95, 175-76
adolescence and, 56-66, 77, 153, 176
anal phase and, 40-46, 75-77, 79
marriage and, 145, 146, 157
Oedipal period and, 48-53, 89-92, 129, 133, 143-44, 153
oral phase and, 36-39, 70-71, 74-75, 78-79
See also Mother-child relationship
Parenthood, 159-76
decision of, 159-63
husband and, 163-65, 173-74
romance and, 186-87
See also Childbearing
Patmore, Coventry, 9-10
Penis, development of, 24
"Penis envy," 18-20, 52
Phallic phase of psychosexual development, 47, 55, 59, 175-76
female, 51-53
male, 47-51
problems in, 82-90
See also Oedipal period
Physiology of reproductive system, 22-34
Pituitary gland and puberty, 25-26, 28-29
Pregnancy, 30-34
deciding on, 159-63
husband and, 163-65
labor and delivery in, 164-65, 171-72
physical changes during, 30-33
Psychoanalysis of self, 96-117
family history and, 100-104
free association and, 112-13, 116, 129, 133-35